DEBATING DEMOCRACY

DEBATING ETHICS

General Editor
Christopher Heath Wellman
Washington University of St. Louis

Debating Ethics is a series of volumes in which leading scholars defend opposing views on timely ethical questions and core theoretical issues in contemporary moral, political, and legal philosophy.

Debating Democracy

Do We Need More or Less?

JASON BRENNAN
AND HÉLÈNE LANDEMORE

OXFORD
UNIVERSITY PRESS

OXFORD
UNIVERSITY PRESS

Oxford University Press is a department of the University of Oxford. It furthers the University's objective of excellence in research, scholarship, and education by publishing worldwide. Oxford is a registered trade mark of Oxford University Press in the UK and certain other countries.

Published in the United States of America by Oxford University Press
198 Madison Avenue, New York, NY 10016, United States of America.

Library of Congress Cataloging-in-Publication Data
Names: Brennan, Jason, 1979- author. | Landemore, Hélène, 1976- author.
Title: Debating democracy : do we need more or less? /
Jason Brennan and Hélène Landemore
Description: New York : Oxford University Press, 2022. |
Series: Debating ethics | Includes bibliographical references and index.
Identifiers: LCCN 2021023444 (print) | LCCN 2021023445 (ebook) |
ISBN 9780197540817 (hardback) | ISBN 9780197540824 (paperback) |
ISBN 9780197540848 (epub)
Subjects: LCSH: Democracy—Philosophy. |
Democracy—Moral and ethical aspects.
Classification: LCC JC423 .B7835 2021 (print) | LCC JC423 (ebook) |
DDC 321.8—dc23
LC record available at https://lccn.loc.gov/2021023444
LC ebook record available at https://lccn.loc.gov/2021023445

DOI: 10.1093/oso/9780197540817.001.0001

CONTENTS

PART 3 RESPONSES

Introduction: How to Fix What Ails Democracy?

WHEN WE WROTE THE FIRST draft of these sentences, pro-democracy protesters in Hong Kong had rallied for six straight months. They demanded safeguards for Hong Kong's political autonomy and universal suffrage for the election of the devolved legislature and chief executive. When we wrote the second draft of this paragraph, it appeared their pro-democratic movement had been crushed.

Democracy is in retreat in a number of countries around the world. In the past decade, Russia, Turkey, and Venezuela transitioned from flawed democracies into authoritarian regimes. Even established democracies experience turmoil. Brexit, the election of Trump, the success of the Five Star Movement in Italy, the prolonged protests against Macron in France, and the rise of extreme parties show that even stable Western democracies are suffering. Is democracy itself, as a normative ideal, in crisis? What other regime could possibly look superior?

Regardless, democracy remains the gold standard form of government. Most people regard democracy as the best and most legitimate form of government. Even dictators

Debating Democracy. Jason Brennan and Hélène Landemore, Oxford University Press. © Oxford University Press 2022. DOI: 10.1093/oso/9780197540817.003.0001

claim to speak for and derive their authority from the people; they go to great pains to imitate democracy including through sham elections.

We agree that the best places to live today are generally well-functioning democracies, rather than sham or partial democracies, one-party states, or something else. We also agree that real-life democracies suffer from significant flaws. We'll debate what we should do about it. Can we, as Landemore argues, fix the problems of democracy with more democracy? Or, as Brennan argues, should we explore alternatives to democracy?

WHAT DO WE MEAN BY "DEMOCRACY"?

We regard a system as democratic to the extent that all members of society share equal fundamental political power. That is an intentionally broad definition. Some regard this definition as too broad—we will consider objections based on this worry later.

This definition includes direct democracies where citizens make the law and indirect or representative democracies where democratic representatives make the law. It includes systems in which majority rule is constrained and unconstrained. We'll start from the common conception of democracy as characterized by universal suffrage, periodic elections, and the peaceful alternation of parties in power, even as we will consider alternative understandings of this regime form (including regimes where political offices are staffed by lottery rather than elections).

American high school students taking Advanced Placement US civics are trained to say, "America is a republic, not a democracy!" This objection insists on using these words in an obsolete way yet it is onto something about the real nature of the American regime. In the late 1700s, political theorists used the word "republic" to refer to representative governments with constitutional limits on their power; they used "democracy" as a pejorative label for mob rule. Today, political scientists and philosophers use the word "democracy" as a broader category to refer to both limited and unlimited representative government with some degree of popular sovereignty. Whether those are real democracies, however, can still be questioned.[1]

Indeed, in practice and by law, no system is perfectly democratic so described. No actual democracy in fact distributes power equally among all members of society. For one thing, not every member of society qualifies as part of the voting public or as a legal citizen. Nearly every democratic government restricts foreign residents from voting. Every country restricts children from voting, usually on the grounds that they do not yet have competent or autonomous political judgment. Many disenfranchise felons or citizens living abroad.

Further, people have unequal ability to run for office. Bernard Manin argued long ago that elections treat citizens unequally as candidates, distributing power to those

---

1. In the same way, in the late 1700s, philosophers used the word "experiment" to refer not to what we would call experiments today (carefully controlled artificial interventions) but to what we would now simply call "observations." Saying today that the US is a republic, not a democracy, is thus like saying that what physicists do are not really experiments, but something else. Words change meaning over time.

with extraordinary, socially salient qualities. In practice, elections tend to empower social and economic elites.[2] In the US, a Kennedy, Clinton, or Bush is far more likely to win office than an average Joe. In most democracies, the rich have more influence de facto than the poor.[3] Majority ethnic groups usually have more effective power and influence than minorities. Handsome candidates tend to beat ugly ones.[4] In the UK, an Oxford grad is more likely to become prime minister than an East Anglia grad. In France, National School of Administration grads are more likely to become president than graduates of regional no-name universities.

WHY *NOT* DEMOCRACY?

We will debate how best to fix democracy, but we also agree that certain arguments for democracy are weak.

Some people say what justifies democracy is fairness: it gives everyone an equal say.

There is an intuitive appeal to this argument. People have fought and died for democracy for this reason. However, it faces serious philosophical problems.

In fact, in real-life democracies, persistent ethnic or ideological minorities often have *no* chance of getting their way. They will always be outvoted. In other words, equal say does not mean equality of influence.

---

2. Manin 1995.
3. Gilens 2012. See also Cagé 2020.
4. Lens and Chappell 2008.

If you genuinely and only wanted to equalize influence, you would not hold elections, which both introduce various kinds of class and racial biases and guarantee unpopular views have no shot. Instead, you would choose decision-makers by lottery, as the ancient Greeks did. For instance, we could pick the president at random from all citizens between the ages 35 and 65. Many think this a bad way to pick a president, but it is perfectly fair: everyone, regardless of class, race, or sex, would have an equal (albeit infinitesimal) chance of being chosen. Or, we could let people vote for candidates, but then assign percentages to each candidate based on the percentage of votes she receives, and, finally, pick winners at random using these weighted percentages. Either system would be far fairer. Whether they would be more desirable is the harder question.

Relatedly, some people say that democracy is just because it treats individuals equally. Giving everyone an equal vote means they are all equals in the eyes of the law.

However, giving everyone an equal vote is but one of many ways we could enshrine and publicly express the ideal of equality. Many liberals of various sorts think the more important way to enshrine equality is to ensure that every person has an extensive and equal set of rights protected by law.

Again, giving everyone an equal vote could undermine other forms of equality. For instance, imagine all white people are virulent racists. Suppose the electorate is 90% white and 10% black. Imagine there are no constitutional restrictions on what laws the society can pass, except that it must remain democratic and everyone must have equal voting rights. Here, the white majority might outvote the black minority and use the law to oppress them, even though each individual white person has the same power as each individual black person.

A closely related argument says that democracy empowers us as individuals. But that seems false, at least in most modern election-based representative democracies. In most elections, how *we* vote matters a great deal, but how any one of us votes matters little. Note that the whole point of democracy is to empower *groups*, not individuals. If how *you* individually voted regularly made much of a difference, then something would be wrong. The probability that an individual vote will make a difference in a typical election is very low.

DEMOCRACY IS GOOD BECAUSE/IF IT WORKS

Instead of those arguments, we think that democracy is good primarily because it works.

Consider, by analogy, a hammer. We value hammers not as ends in themselves, but because they do a job. We would not insist on using an inferior hammer over a better hammer. We would not insist on using a hammer when we need a wrench.

For the purposes of this book, this is how we'll evaluate democracy. We put aside questions about whether democracy is an end in itself or valuable for what it expresses. Instead, we debate whether democracy is the best tool for the job.

Let's introduce a technical term. "Instrumentalism" refers to a set of views about what justifies having one form of government over another. Instrumentalists hold:

1. There are procedure-independent right answers to at least some political questions. To illustrate, think of a criminal jury trying to assess whether someone is guilty. There is an independent fact that they are trying to discover. This is in contrast with, say, a game of dice, where the "right" answer is procedurally defined: whoever rolls the highest number wins.

2. What justifies the distribution of power, or a particular way of making political decisions, is (at least in part) that this distribution or method tends to get the right answer.

To continue with the jury example, we can ask whether other trial decisions are more reliable, overall. Which procedure is most likely to get us to the truth of the matter about whether the accused committed the crime? Perhaps a tribunal of judges or an AI bot would be superior.

We might also worry that some systems have too high a chance of selecting horrible answers. Aristotle argued that the main virtue of republican forms of government is not that they tend to pick the best policies, but that they rarely pick very disastrous policies. In contrast, he thought monarchies were more likely to pick excellent policies, but also more likely to pick disastrous policies. He thought republicanism was best because it minimized the risk of very bad outcomes, even at the expense of a reduced chance of exceptionally good outcomes.

We both agree that we should judge democracy primarily by how well it serves the ends of the polity, whether defined as justice, stability, efficiency, or some other value. Or, more abstractly, by how well it works.

We reject a strange moral relativism that certain democrats accept. In Plato's *Euthyphro*, Socrates asks Euthyphro whether things are good because the gods say so or whether the gods say those things are good *because* they are good. There must be some underlying reason why some things are good and others evil; they are not good or evil simply because Zeus decided they are on a whim. Similarly, we agree that what makes many things good or bad in a democracy is that they are good or bad for independent reasons, not because a democracy judges them to be so. If 95% of people vote to do something evil, awful, or stupid, it remains evil, awful, and stupid.

We both think democracy should be judged primarily by its results. We reject the view that people can always just decide, by fiat, what counts as good results. But then, you should ask, what counts as good results? Here, we will try to rest our cases on the broad values and goals that people across the world tend to share, such as human rights protection, economic prosperity, peace, security, basic dignity, individual freedom, education, health, and general individual well-being.

How to weigh all these values when they conflict is a hard question. The good news is that we doubt we'll need to do that to make our arguments go through. Instead, we'll discuss certain features of democracy, aggregative voting, deliberation, voter psychology, political incentives, and so on, and explain why we have independent reasons to think these phenomena are likely to track the truth about the common good of a given polity and lead to good decisions, or not.

In the same way, a philosopher of science—or your middle school science teacher—can explain to you why using scientific methods are generally reliable and trustworthy ways to track the truth, without having to first tell you what all of the truths of science are. We can explain to you why wishful thinking, in contrast, is not a reliable guide to truth in mathematics without first having to discover all the truths of math. In this book, for the most part, we can debate whether certain political decision-making methods are reliable or not based upon outside evidence, but without having to pin our arguments on our particular political views. We will occasionally use some specific examples where we think democracy got the right or wrong answer, but our arguments will rarely hinge on these specific examples.

Of course, when we ask whether democracy is reliable, we have to ask, compared to what? Our answer: compared to the feasible alternatives; that is, compared to other forms of government that could be implemented given the constraints of human nature. In this book, we're not interested in asking what the *ideal* form of government would be, if only everyone were a moral saint who always did the right thing. We want to know which political regime will best tend to make good decisions and produce good outcomes, given that people's willingness and ability to comply with institutions are imperfect, given that people are sometimes incompetent and corrupt, and given that institutions are not guaranteed to work as intended.

BRENNAN: DEMOCRACY WITHOUT ROMANCE

In the opening chapter, Brennan will argue the reasons most people accept democracy are nearly irrelevant to real-world democracies. Their mental model of democracy does not match how democracies in fact perform or could be made to perform under realistic circumstances. They think citizens form their political affiliations on the basis of their background beliefs and values. When citizens vote, they support politicians who will advance their favored ideas. In the end, democracies deliver, if not the will of the people, at least a compromise position among their separate wills. In contrast, he'll argue, the empirical work shows that most citizens lack any stable ideology or political beliefs, and their political affiliations are largely arbitrary. Their votes do not communicate their genuine support for different policies or values. Citizens are ignorant, misinformed, and tribalistic despite lacking firm beliefs. As a result, the more power we give them, the more we suffer the consequences. Whatever we say about democracy, we need to be realistic about how people behave.

In chapter 2, Brennan will note that most philosophers try to "solve" these problems by arguing we need more and better democracy. In particular, they think certain kinds of democratic systems could unleash the hidden "wisdom of the crowds." However, he'll argue, they either rely upon mistaken applications of certain mathematical theorems, or they end up retreating toward unrealistic ideals of how people *ought* to behave. In effect, they say that democracy *would* be wonderful if only people behaved the right way.

But, he'll argue, there is no realistic mechanism to get them to behave the right way.

In chapter 3, Brennan will argue that part of the solution is to reduce the sphere of politics and also the sphere of political control. Certain issues, such as trade policy, immigration policy, central banking interest rates, who serves as district attorney or judge, and various kinds of regulation, should be kept out of citizens' hands, for everybody's own good.

In chapter 4, Brennan will argue that we should be open to experimenting with certain non-democratic forms of government. In particular, he'll argue that Enlightened Preference Voting is likely to be superior to our current system. In Enlightened Preference Voting, all citizens may vote. When they vote, they (1) register their preferences, (2) indicate their demographic categories, and (3) take a short test of basic, easily verifiable political knowledge. Afterward, all three sets of "data" are anonymized and made public. The government—and any decent political scientist or newspaper—can then calculate what a demographically identical public *would* have supported if only everyone got a perfect score on the test. He'll argue that while such a system would be subject to special interest rent-seeking, it is nevertheless likely to be superior to any realistic democracy as we find it.

LANDEMORE: LET'S TRY REAL DEMOCRACY

In her first chapter, chapter 5, Landemore will put forward a general theoretical case for the benefits of distributing political decision-power in an inclusive and egalitarian manner and for locating the legitimacy of laws and policies in the deliberations of the people or their democratic representatives. The core idea is that many minds are better than few to deal with the uncertainty and complexity of the world and figuring out solutions that work for all in it. This argument builds on the formal properties of two key decision-making mechanisms of democracy, namely inclusive deliberation on equal grounds and majority rule with universal suffrage. Properly used in sequence and under the right conditions, these two mechanisms ensure that no information and viewpoint is ignored and maximize the cognitive diversity brought to bear on collective political problems and predictions. Building on existing formal results by Lu Hong and Scott Page, the chapter introduces the "Numbers Trump Ability" theorem, which formalizes the intuition that many minds are smarter than just a few. Under the right conditions systems governed by democratic decision-procedures can be expected to deliver greater epistemic performance than less inclusive and egalitarian systems.

In chapter 6, Landemore addresses theoretical and empirical objections to the epistemic argument for democracy presented in the previous chapter (the argument from collective wisdom). The objections this chapter addresses include those based on the average voter's alleged incompetence and systematic biases, as well as those that challenge the relevance of deductive arguments for democracy. The main counterpoint is that focusing on individual input into the democratic process to infer the quality of democratic outcomes (the model "garbage in, garbage out" used by Brennan) is misguided. It fails to consider that collective intelligence is an emergent property that crucially depends on group properties not captured by measures of individual input. Systematic biases would be, and often are, a problem for democracy but no more than for oligarchies of knowers. In a free and diverse public sphere the public and its democratic representatives have more opportunities to debias themselves, at least over time, than small groups of homogenously thinking elites.

In chapter 7, Landemore argues against both oligarchic and majoritarian rule by knowers, or epistocracies. Such regimes are necessarily blind to a number of interests and perspectives, rendering them epistemically inferior to fully inclusive democracies over the long term. The chapter first consider the classic defense of Chinese-style epistocracy by Daniel Bell and then turns to the more puzzling rule by the knowledgeable 95% defended by Jason Brennan. While Bell's Chinese model is much more vulnerable to epistemic failure due to the blindspots it structurally builds in its decision-process, even Brennan's majoritarian epistocracy takes the unjustifiable epistemic risk of silencing what could be the most relevant voices on crucial issues.

In chapter 8, Landemore returns to the ideal of people's power and argues that democracies as we know them are dubiously democratic. Most ordinary citizens in existing representative democracies have little deliberative input into the laws and policies that rule their lives. The chapter traces the problem to fundamental design mistakes made in the eighteenth century when elections, an oligarchic selection mechanism, rather than the traditional lot of Classical Athens, were privileged as the method for choosing representatives. This chapter also makes the case for open democracy, a new paradigm of democracy inspired by a number of real-life experiments in participatory democracy and in which the center of power is accessible to all citizens on an equal basis. Central to this new paradigm are new forms of democratic representation that are truly inclusive and egalitarian, such as open mini-publics connected to the larger population via crowdsourcing platforms and moments of mass voting.

Part 1

BRENNAN—DEMOCRACY

WITHOUT ROMANCE

Chapter 1

How Real Democracy Really Works

"REAL SOCIALISM HAS NEVER BEEN TRIED"

Roughly ninety countries in the twentieth century experimented with centrally planned socialist economies. None of them got rich. Roughly the same number experimented with market-based economies, and all of them got richer, and got richer in proportion to how market-oriented they were. This seems instructive. Markets went ninety for ninety; socialism, zero for ninety.

Despite that, many still advocate socialism. Why?

Many socialists employ a rhetorical trick that insulates their ideology from any damning empirical evidence. When you show them how bad things were in those ninety countries, they respond, "That wasn't *real* socialism."

Oddly, "real socialism" is always imaginary socialism. Socialism counts as *real* only when it matches the idealized description of socialism in theorists' heads. In real socialism, the society must implement the rules

Debating Democracy. Jason Brennan and Hélène Landemore, Oxford University Press. © Oxford University Press 2022. DOI: 10.1093/oso/9780197540817.003.0002

exactly as the theorist imagines; people always have the proper motivations, desires, and attitudes; and people always behave the right way. A real socialist society is thus one where the theorist stipulates what the rules are, how people will respond to the rules, and what the outcomes will be. Since no actual socialist society matches their imagination, then no actual socialist societies count as real.

Democrats often do the same thing. Political philosophers and theorists who specialize in democratic theory often have a quasi-religious reverence for democracy. But they often defend an *idealized description* of democracy against what they regard as realistic descriptions of the alternatives. They are uninterested in defending democracy as we find it. They often say, "That's not *real* democracy." Just as socialists say, "Real socialism has never been tried," they say, "real democracy has never been tried," rather than conclude that perhaps real human beings are unable or unwilling to make democracy work.

I regard democracy as the best political system so far. But it works only when kept in its rightful place and properly constrained. A large range of issues—such as the operation of central banks or what the price of corn will be—should be kept away from democratic control. Further, despite all its virtues, democracy has serious built-in flaws and injustices. Injustice remains unjust even when democracy does it. We should not tolerate injustice when we don't have to, and we shouldn't ignore it because our favorite political system does it. We should be open to experimenting with non-democratic alternatives that might reduce democracy's problems.

YOUR SIXTH GRADE CIVICS TEACHER WAS WRONG

US students often take civics around sixth grade. Sixth-grade civics offers a basic model of how democracy is supposed to work. Most college students, radio and TV journalists, and politically active citizens accept this model. Let's review the sixth-grade model.

First, the model holds that citizens know their various interests and concerns. This doesn't necessarily mean that citizens are selfish or entirely self-interested.

Second, the model holds that citizens learn how the world works, how government works, how the economy functions, and so on. After learning some facts—and some of the social scientific theories they need to understand these facts or predict cause and effect—citizens form preferences about the policies they wish to implement. They adopt an ideology: an *organized and coherent set of political principles*. Some citizens are more conservative and others more liberal. Some want smaller government, some want bigger. Some want government to enforce traditional morality, others to enforce social justice, while some want it to enforce minimal morals.

Third, citizens learn about the political parties and candidates. They tend to vote for the candidates and parties they most agree with. If their best match has little chance of winning, they might vote strategically for those with better chances, or they might abstain.

Parties and politicians know that appealing to voters is necessary to win power. Thus, what voters want determines what the parties offer. Leading candidates tend to be in the center of active voters' ideological and policy preferences.

Fourth, because of this, after the election, lawmakers pass new laws, regulations, and policies that reflect citizens' overall ideological preferences, or at least reflect a kind of compromise among all their disparate preferences.

Fifth, come the next election, citizens judge how well the lawmakers and other elected officials performed. If lawmakers failed to keep their promises, if they did a bad job, if they were corrupt and unethical, or if the policies they implemented (even if they were what the people wanted) produced bad results, citizens will hold officials accountable by voting against the bad performers and voting in favor of the good performers. The technical term for this behavior is "retrospective voting."

To summarize the sixth-grade model of democracy in diagram form:

> Individual interests → policy and outcome preferences → party affiliation/candidate preferences and electoral results → policy results → retrospective voting

If the sixth-grade model were correct, it would at least partly justify democracy on instrumentalist grounds. Democracy makes governments do what the people want, and what the people want is good for them.

Even if this model were correct, we could still invoke the classic worry that an unchecked democracy enables the majority to ignore, push around, or even exploit the minority. We might also invoke the modern worry, studied extensively by public choice economists, that extended bureaucracies with devolved powers tend to serve special interests rather than serve the common good.[1]

But the bigger problem is that sixth-grade civics offers an obsolete, largely falsified model of democracy. Today we know that every piece of this model is highly exaggerated or mistaken. It is not a good approximation or simplification of real-life political behavior.

We need a better model. But once we get it, the classic argument for democracy disappears. Elections are not a mechanism by which politicians are forced to serve citizens' considered interests and goals.

THE PEOPLE KNOW NOTHING

In the 1950s, political scientists began surveying random samples of citizens, including citizens who regularly vote, trying to determine how much citizens know.

As political scientist Philip Converse summarizes, "The two simplest truths I know about the distribution of political information in modern electorates are that the mean is low and the variance is high."[2] Legal theorist Ilya Somin, author of *Democracy and Political Ignorance*, says, "The sheer depth of most individual voters' ignorance is shocking to many observers not familiar with the research."[3] Political scientist Larry Bartels says, "The political ignorance of the

1. Mueller 2003.
2. Converse 1990, 372.
3. Somin 2013, 17.

American voter is one the best-documented features of contemporary politics."[4] Political scientist John Ferejohn agrees: "Nothing strikes the student of public opinion and democracy more forcefully than the paucity of information most people possess about politics."[5]

The typical citizen, and even the modal voter, is ignorant of most basic political information.[6] American citizens are unaware of most major recent policy changes, do not know what is in the federal budget, cannot estimate major economic or social indicators (such as unemployment or crime rates) with any degree of precision, and have little idea what different parties or candidates have done or propose to do.[7] Even during election years, most citizens cannot identify any congressional candidates in their district.[8] Citizens generally don't know which party controls Congress.[9]

Voters use words such as "liberal" and "conservative," but do not seem to know what the words signify. For instance, during the 2000 US presidential election, slightly more than half of all Americans correctly identified that Al Gore was more liberal than George W. Bush. Yet only 57% of them knew Gore favored a higher level of government

4. Bartels 1996, 194.
5. Ferejohn 1990, 3.
6. Campbell et al. 1960; Delli-Carpini & Keeter 1996; Converse 1964; Friedman 2006; Caplan 2007; Somin 2013; Brennan 2016.
7. Delli-Carpini and Keeter 1996; Somin 2013; Brennan 2016a.
8. Hardin 2009, 60.
9. Somin 2013, 17–21.

spending than Bush did, while significantly fewer than half knew that Gore was more supportive of abortion rights, was more supportive of welfare-state programs, favored a higher degree of aid to blacks, or was more supportive of environmental regulation.[10] Only 37% knew that federal spending on the poor had increased or that crime had decreased in the 1990s.[11] On these questions, Americans did worse than a coin flip. Similar results hold for other election years.[12]

Surveys of basic political knowledge generally *overestimate* how much citizens know. One reason is that they usually take the form of multiple-choice tests. We can't distinguish between those who knew the answer from those who made a lucky guess.

These surveys also focus on *basic* political information, such as the size of the budget, the unemployment rate, or recent political history. They don't survey whether citizens know basic economics or political science, have any ability to understand these basic facts, understand how politics works, or can determine how policies work or which policies cause which outcomes.

Between one third to half of citizens are political know-nothings. In some countries, people know a little more; in others, a little less. But the median, mean, and modal citizen is innocent of the basic information they need to vote well.

---

10. Somin 2013, 31.
11. Somin 2013, 32.
12. E.g., Althaus 2003, 11.

THE PEOPLE OFTEN KNOW LESS
THAN NOTHING

Voters are not merely ignorant, but often systematically misinformed. They do not simply fail to know the facts, but often also have false beliefs.

For instance, during the Brexit vote, UK citizens vastly overestimated the number of EU immigrants in the UK, overestimated Chinese foreign investment, dramatically underestimated EU investment in the UK, and vastly overestimated how much the UK sends to the EU in terms of various welfare payments.[13] Leave voters overestimated the number of European immigrants by a factor of 4, underestimated the amount of foreign investment by a factor of 50, and overestimated the amount of money leaving the UK for EU welfare programs by a factor of 100.[14] Perhaps if they knew the correct numbers, they would have voted differently.

The American National Election Studies generally find that the least informed quartile of voters are systematically misinformed. For instance, in the 1992 American National Election Study, voters were asked to identify which party, the Democrats or Republicans, was more conservative on average. Only 12% of people in the lowest

13. https://www.ipsos-mori.com/researchpublications/
researcharchive/3742/The-Perils-of-Perception-and-
the-EU.aspx
14. https://www.ipsos-mori.com/researchpublications/
researcharchive/3742/The-Perils-of-Perception-and-
the-EU.aspx

knowledge quartile could do so. They were also asked to identify the relative ideological positions of the two major party candidates (sitting president) George Bush or Bill Clinton. Only 17.9% of people in the lowest knowledge quartile could do so. Only 17.1% of them could identify which candidate, Clinton or Bush, was more pro-choice. Only 9.7% of them could identify which candidate, Clinton or Bush, wanted to expand government services or the welfare state more.[15]

THE PEOPLE DO NOT ENGAGE IN RETROSPECTIVE VOTING

The sixth-grade model holds that We the People will vote the bastards out if the bastards do a bad job. Unfortunately, there is little evidence for this hypothesis.

In reality, retrospective voting is a difficult task that requires tremendous information and social scientific expertise. You need to know who was in office. You need to know what they did and what they could have done. You need to determine cause and effect, for instance, to determine whether the current recession resulted from forces in or beyond a particular politician's or party's control. You need to know who the challengers are and whether they are likely to perform better. All this requires tremendous knowledge of the facts, of cause and effect, of counterfactuals and the inner workings of government.

15. Althaus 2003, 11.

Generally, voters have little sense of who was in power or what those people could do.[16] They do not know what influence incumbents had, or how to attribute responsibility to different incumbents.[17] They often do not even know whether things got better or worse. For instance, crime—one of the biggest problems in the United States throughout the 1970s and 80s—fell dramatically during Bill Clinton's tenure, but most Americans believed it increased. During the 2012 election, most Americans did not know that the economy grew rather than shrank the year before.[18]

Political scientists Christopher Achen and Larry Bartels have carefully measured the degree to which voters respond to past economic trends when assessing how to vote. They find that voters do, in fact, punish incumbents if the economy is doing badly. However, voters only remember and react to the past six months of economic performance, rather than assessing the economy as a whole in the incumbents' terms.

But, Achen and Bartels caution, this does not show voters are *good* at retrospection, if only for the short term. Instead, voters punish or reward incumbents for the past sixth months, regardless of to what degree, if any, the incumbent was responsible for them. It's like voters kick the dog because they had a bad day at work.[19]

16. Caplan, Crampton, Grove, and Somin 2013.
17. Caplan, Crampton, Grove, and Somin 2013; Healy and Malholtra 2010.
18. Somin 2013, 18–21.
19. Achen and Bartels 2016.

INFORMATION CHANGES
POLICY PREFERENCES

Ignorance and misinformation would not matter if they had no effect on how people vote. But, in fact, information changes what people want. High-information and low-information people have systematically different policy preferences (when they have any preferences at all). The difference is explained by information and not by confounding factors.

Don't confuse well informed with *educated*. Education, once we control for other confounds, has only a small independent effect on voters' political knowledge.[20]

Suppose we poll all the well-informed and badly informed people and discover significant political disagreement. This might result from differential knowledge or some other factor. For instance, due to racism and oppression, political knowledge is not evenly distributed among all demographic groups. In general, members of privileged demographic groups are better informed than others.[21] Accordingly, we might worry that if the well informed and the badly informed disagree about politics, this reflects not

---

20. Somin 2013, 171–178.
21. Althaus 2003, 16; Delli Carpini and Keeter 1996, 135–177. E.g., less than 40% of all blacks can identify which political party was more conservative, but the majority of whites can (Delli Carpini and Keeter 1996, 166). On the 1988 survey, high-income older men get average scores that are nearly three times as high as the average score of low-income black women (Delli Carpini and Keeter 1996, 162; see also Delli Carpini and Keeter 1991; Neuman 1986; Palfrey and Poole 1987; Althaus 1998).

different information but different interests based on different demographics.

Fortunately, scholars researching this topic have already investigated it. The way political scientists and economists control for confounding factors is to collect multiple sets of data:

1. What people want (which policies they support, what goals they prioritize, which candidates they support).
2. Who the people are (race, sex, gender, income, employment status, where they live, etc.).
3. What they know.

With these three sets of data, one can determine the independent effect of information (or ignorance or misinformation) on policy preferences while statistically controlling for the effects of demographics. For instance, when we see that well-informed people (who also tend to be richer) favor free trade while ignorant people (who also tend to be poorer) favor protectionism, we now know it's the information rather than income that explains the difference.[22]

With this method, political scientist Scott Althaus also finds, using the American National Election Studies data, that well-informed and badly informed citizens have systematically different policy preferences.[23] Althaus finds that poorly informed people have systematically different preferences from well-informed people, even after we

22. Caplan 2007.
23. Althaus 2003, 129; Caplan 2007. Both Althaus and Caplan correct for the influence of demographic factors.

correct for the influence of demographic factors, such as race, income, and gender. As people (regardless of their race, income, gender, or other demographic factors) become more informed, they favor overall less government intervention and control of the economy. (That's not to say they become libertarians.) They are more in favor of free trade and less in favor of protectionism. They are more pro-choice. They favor using tax increases to offset the deficit and debt. They favor less punitive and harsh measures on crime. They are less hawkish on military policy, though they favor other forms of intervention. They are more accepting of affirmative action. They are less supportive of prayer in public schools. They are more supportive of market solutions to health-care problems. They are less moralistic in law; they don't want government to impose morality on the population. And so on. In contrast, people who are less informed are more in favor of protectionism, abortion restrictions, harsh penalties on crime, doing nothing to fix the debt, more hawkish intervention, and so on. Other studies use different data sets and find similar results.[24]

Political scientist Martin Gilens finds similar results inside the Democratic Party. Low-information Democrats are more strongly in favor of the Patriot Act, of invasions of civil liberty, torture, protectionism, and restricting abortion rights and access to birth control. They are less tolerant of homosexuals and more opposed to gay rights.[25] High-information Democrats have the opposite preferences. They tend to have opposed the Iraq invasion and

---

24. Bartels 1996; Caplan 2007; Gilens 2012.
25. Gilens 2012, 106–111.

torture, support free trade, civil liberties, gay rights, abortion rights, and access to birth control.

Above, I noted that both Leave and Brexit voters were systematically misinformed about the basic facts germane to the Brexit vote. However, the Leave voters were systematically *more* misinformed than the Remain voters.

Economist Bryan Caplan notes that laypeople and economists have systematically different opinions about economic issues. For instance, consider the Survey of Americans and Economists on the Economy (SAEE), conducted in 1996 by the *Washington Post*, Kaiser Family Foundation, and Harvard University Survey Project. When asked why the economy was not doing better, the public thought "there are too many immigrants" was between a minor to major reason, while economists thought it was no reason at all. The public thought "technology is displacing workers," "business profits are too high," "companies are sending jobs overseas," and "companies are downsizing" were reasons why the economy was not doing better, while economists did not.[26]

Of course, economists are demographically distinct from the population at large. Perhaps their demographics rather than their economics training explains the differences of opinion. To test this hypothesis, Caplan borrows Althaus's statistical methods. He finds that the differences are explained not by demographics, but by economics training. Compared to economists, the lay public

---

26. Caplan 2007, 61–66. See also *Washington Post*, Kaiser Family Foundation, and Harvard University Survey Project, "Survey of Americans and Economists on the Economy," #1199 October 16, 2006.

systematically underestimates how well markets perform, systematically underestimates the value of trade and immigration, and is systematically pessimistic about the future.[27]

THE DANGERS OF MISINFORMATION

The quality of candidates and of party platforms depends in part on which citizens are likely to vote, what they are like, how they reason, and what they want. Politicians and parties want to win elections. They create platforms and run candidates that they believe will mobilize voters on their behalf.

For instance, the familiar median voter theorem claims that parties have a strong incentive to push the policies preferred by the median voter. If the median voter is foolish, then parties would push foolish policies. If the median voter is enlightened and well informed, then parties would push good policies.

I don't mean to argue that median voter theorem is correct—or assert it isn't. Rather, it illustrates a broader point: Who runs depends on who votes. What they run depends on who votes. Just *how* responsive the quality of the candidates is to the quality of the voters is up for debate. The empirical literature does not settle this question. If people form ideologies or vote on the basis of misinformation, and if politicians respond to their ideological preferences, we should be worried.

27. Caplan 2007.

THE PEOPLE ARE IRRATIONAL ABOUT POLITICS

Studies in political psychology overwhelmingly find that citizens do not reason about politics in a scientific or truth-tracking way. Rather, voters engage in motivated reasoning; they tend to believe what they want to believe rather than what the evidence supports.

For instance, they suffer from both confirmation bias (they tend only to seek out, to pay attention to, and to accept information that reinforces their current beliefs) and disconfirmation bias (they tend to reject or ignore information that undermines their current beliefs). When confronted with evidence *against* their current views, they tend to respond by digging in their heels and believing their current views more strongly. They suffer from affect contagion and prior attitude effects; their occurrent emotional states change how they process new information. They suffer from framing effects; the opinions they offer in response to questions depend on the wording of those questions, and they will switch answers if offered a logically identical question that replaces one word with a synonym.[28]

---

28. Tversky and Kahneman 1973; Kahneman, Slovic, and Tversky 1982; Rasinki 1989; Bartels 2003; Arceneaux and Stein 2006;; Westen et al. 2006; Westen 2008; Kelly 2012; Haidt 2012; Chong 2013; Lodge and Taber 2013; Taber and Young 2013; Erison, Lodge, and Tabor 2014.

THE PEOPLE ARE NOT IDEOLOGICAL AND YET VERY TRIBALISTIC

Many voters describe themselves as "liberal" or "conservative," but research generally finds that most lack organized or stable sets of political beliefs. Most have few political opinions, and even fewer stable opinions; what few opinions they have cannot be amalgamated into a coherent position.[29]

In *Neither Liberal nor Conservative*, Donald Kinder and Nathan Kalmoe review the vast empirical literature on voter opinion, including their own. They estimate that fewer than 1 out of 5 voters have something like a political ideology.[30] Plenty of other research finds similar results.[31] Further, contrary to popular myth, there are few "single-issue" voters.[32] In general, cognitive

---

29. Converse 1964; Barnes 1971; Inglehart and Klingemann 1976; Arian and Shamir 1983; Converse and Pierce 1986; Zaller 1992; McCann 1997; Goren 2005; Zechmeister 2006; Lewis-Beck et al. 2008; Achen and Bartels 2016; Kinder and Kalmoe 2017; Mason 2017; Mason 2018.
30. Kinder and Kalmoe 2017.
31. Mason 2018; Achen and Bartels 2016; Jardina 2019; Mason and Wronski 2018; Barber and Pope 2018; McCarty 2019.
32. Converse 1964; Barnes 1971; Inglehart and Klingemann 1976; Arian and Shamir 1983; Converse and Pierce 1986; Bartels 1986; Zaller 1992; McCann 1997; Goren 2005; Zechmeister 2006; Muddle 2007; Lewis-Beck et al. 2008; Achen and Bartels 2016; Kinder and Kalmoe 2017; Mason 2018.

elites have ideologies and vote on the basis of ideology, but the majority of voters identify with parties on non-ideological grounds, and simply vote the same way every time.

Though most voters are not ideological, voters still suffer from "intergroup bias." They see themselves as part of a political team. They are generous and forgiving of members of their own political team, while they tend to presume that supporters of rival political parties are stupid, selfish, and morally corrupt.[33] They prefer to live among people who share their political identity, and tend to dislike, mistreat, and discriminate against those with different political identities.[34] They want their political team to win, but most of them do not genuinely support what their party supports.[35]

If voters were ideological, this tribalism might reflect moral differences. Voters hate each other because they have conflicting views about fundamental justice. However, the antipathy between most voters is more like the antipathy between fans of different sports teams. The typical Republican or Democratic voter is ideologically innocent yet convinced the other voter wants to destroy the country.

33. Mutz 2006; Chong 2013.
34. Tajfel and Turner 1979; Tajfel 1981; Tajfel 1982; Cohen 2003; Mutz 2006; Iyengar et al. 2012; Kahan et al. 2013; Somin 2013; Iyengar and Westwood 2015.
35. Mason 2018.

PEOPLE VOTE FOR WHO THEY ARE, NOT WHAT THEY WANT

Kwame Anthony Appiah says, "People don't vote for what they want. They vote for who they are."[36] This is an excellent one-sentence summary of the theory called *democratic realism*.

The sixth-grade model of voter behavior holds that citizens first have goals, then form political beliefs about what will best realize those goals, then vote for the parties that share their beliefs. There is strong evidence this is true for only a small subset of voters. It's more common for causation to go the other way. Rather than people voting Democrat because they share the Democrat's ideology, it's more common that people share the Democrat's ideology because they vote Democrat.

Achen and Bartels argue that citizens vote largely on the basis of partisan loyalties. These partisan loyalties are grounded in their identities, but do not track ideology, sincere policy preferences, or their interests. Rather, partisan attachments usually result from accidental, historical connections between certain identity groups and certain political movements and parties. Certain groups become attached to certain parties, but not because they believe in what those parties do or because those parties tend best to serve their interests and goals. Various identities or demographic groups become attached to particular

---

36. https://www.washingtonpost.com/outlook/people-dont-vote-for-want-they-want-they-vote-for-who-they-are/2018/08/30/fb5b7e44-abd7-11e8-8a0c-70b618c98d3c_story.html?utm_term=.b8109bf6cbb6

political parties for largely *accidental* historical events or circumstances that have little to do with voters' underlying values or interests.[37] For example, American Jews switched from Republican to Democratic loyalties between 1928 and 1940, not because of policy platform changes, the Wall Street Crash, or ideological changes, but because of reduced antagonism between Jews and Catholics in the 1930s.[38] Most citizens simply lack underlying ideological commitments or significant political views.

By analogy, a person from Boston becomes a Red Sox and Patriots fan because that is what Bostonians do. They wear Pats shirts to signal or express to one another they are a loyal part of a particular network, and so can be trusted as potential business partners, mates, or neighbors.

For most citizens, political affiliation is psychologically equivalent to sports team loyalty. Their political affiliations are little more reflective of their moral views, views of justice, or views of the good life than their commitment to the Red Sox or Patriots. Their political behavior reflects their demographic identities (such as "Boston Irish" or "evangelical Christian"). Most citizens possess some regulating self-identity (which may be complex), such as "college professor" or "Boston Irish" or "Southern evangelical Christian." Politically active citizens learn how others with the same regulating identity vote, and then usually vote the same way.[39]

---

37. Achen and Bartels 2016, 213–266; Campbell et al. 1960; Tajfel 1982; Greene 1999; Gamm 1989.
38. Achen and Bartels 2016, 236–240.
39. Somin 2013; Achen and Bartels 2016; Simler and Hanson 2018; Mason 2018.

On the realist picture, most voters stop here. Voters generally lack political beliefs. However, a sizeable minority of citizens do express commitments to ideologies and political beliefs. However, realists claim, for most of these seemingly ideological citizens, there is little more than a post-hoc, superficial endorsement of their party's platform. These voters learn what their party stands for and claim/convince themselves that they also stand for it. These voters have no deep, interest-based commitment to their party's ideology. They will express commitment to it, but most will immediately express commitment to a new platform or ideology if their party changes, unaware that they have even "changed their minds." They will claim they have always believed these new or opposite opinions.[40]

The evidence for the realist hypothesis is multifold. First, we have evidence that most people simply lack ideology, despite their persistent voting for one side or the other.[41] Second, we see, as mentioned above, that people "change their minds" when their party changes platforms, but are not aware of the change. For instance, most Republicans who claim to have an opinion on trade switched almost overnight from pro–free trade to protectionist when Trump became the presumptive nominee. Third, we see the clustering of political beliefs around whatever the party happens to endorse. As Dan Kahan summarizes:

40. Achen and Bartels 2016, 267–296; see also Lenz 2009; Lenz 2012.
41. Kinder and Kalmoe 2017; Mason 2017; Mason 2018.

Whether humans are heating the earth and concealed-carry laws increase crime, moreover, turn on wholly distinct bodies of evidence. There is no logical reason for positions on these two empirical issues—not to mention myriad others, including the safety of underground nuclear-waste disposal, the deterrent impact of the death penalty, the efficacy of invasive forms of surveillance to combat terrorism to cluster at all, much less form packages of beliefs that so strongly unite citizens of one set of outlooks and divide those of opposing ones. However, there is a psychological explanation. . . . That explanation is politically motivated reasoning."[42]

These issues are logically independent of each other, yet if you take a stance on one issue, we can predict with near certainty what stance you have on all the others. The best explanation for this is that—among the minority of voters who even have policy preferences—people adopt whatever their party's stance is. They advocate policies because their party advocates them; they do not choose a party because they share its policy ideas.

Realists accept that a small minority of voters are genuinely ideological, with sincere political beliefs and with political affiliation based on such beliefs. This minority fits the populist model above. The sixth-grade model is not entirely wrong, but it applies only to a tiny fraction of citizens, especially to elites. It is the exception to the rule rather than the rule.

42. Kahan 2016.

HEURISTICS AND SHORTCUTS
DON'T SAVE THE DAY

Some democratic theorists say the problems of ignorance and irrationality are not so bad, because voters can simply use heuristics to determine how to vote.[43] They can follow their friends or follow thought leaders. For instance, I'm no expert on fine dining, but I can follow Tyler Cowen's ethnic dining guide for DC (slogan: "All food is ethnic food."). I don't know much about philosophy of religion, but I can ask my colleague Mark for guidance. And so on. Perhaps citizens can also follow the lead of their friends, a political party leader, or a policy expert.

The trouble is, people's selection of heuristics is determined by their tribalistic and partisan political biases.[44] Republicans and Democrats, regardless of how ideological they are (remember that most are not ideological) simply select the "thought leaders" in their tribe and follow their lead. Moreover, people's perception of who counts as an expert is similarly warped by politically motivated reasoning.[45] Of course, a citizen may always roll up their sleeves and do what's needed to arrive at an unbiased and well-informed judgment of which heuristics to trust. But now they've defeated the purpose of using a heuristic, which was to spare them the cost of doing their own epistemic work.[46] At any rate, the available empirical work on shortcuts and heuristics does not support a triumphant view;

43. Lupia and McCubbins 1998; Christiano 2015, 257–260.
44. Somin 2013, 99–100.
45. Kahan et al. 2011.
46. Somin 2013, 99.

instead, it seems that high-information and highly ideo-logical voters can use heuristics well, but others (i.e., the majority) can't.[47]

If anything, this understates the heuristics problem. After all, if most voters support their parties for non-ideological, non-policy-based, non-interest-based reasons, then it's unclear what it would even mean to use a shortcut or heuristic. Bob voting Republican because all his friends do doesn't show that Bob found an easy way to vote for his ideology or interests. Bob doesn't have an ideology and doesn't vote to further political ends. There are no short-cuts because Bob doesn't even have a destination.

DEMOCRACY HAS A BAD INCENTIVE PROBLEM

It is largely uncontroversial in political science that citizens are ignorant and often misinformed. It is uncontrover-sial in political psychology that citizens reason in biased, unscientific ways, and overwhelmingly engage in moti-vated reasoning. The claim that most citizens are not ideo-logical enjoys robust and growing support in light of recent research, which seems to vindicate Philip Converse. The realist view that citizens adopt parties for non-cognitive, non-ideological reasons is widely supported, but more controversial.

Why are people like this? The most commonly accepted explanation is that people are *rationally ignorant* and

47. Colombo and Steenbergen 2020.

rationally irrational. Voters respond rationally to the perverse incentives democracy creates.

Imagine you are in an organic chemistry class with 1000 students. Suppose the professor announces, "Everyone will take one final exam in fourteen weeks, worth 100% of their grade. Rather than each student receiving her individual test result, I will average the tests together. You will each receive the same grade."

You'd expect the average grade would be an F. Hardly anyone would study. After all, your individual effort would barely nudge the average. For instance, if the class average is 30/100 without you, then even if you score 100 on the test, your final grade would be 30.07. In this case, unless you had some other use for the knowledge, it would be *rational* for you to remain ignorant of organic chemistry.

Democratic elections are like taking a final exam, every four years, on moral philosophy, political science, economics, sociology, and current events. Rather than having 999 fellow students, you have tens or hundreds of millions. If you study hard, discover the truths about justice, economics, and politics, and vote accordingly . . . the same result occurs as if you had studied not at all and voted the other way . . . . and the same result occurs if you don't vote at all. You won't change the outcome of the election, you won't change the "mandate," and you won't change what the winning candidates do.

A person is said to be *rationally ignorant* when she fails to acquire or retain information because the expected costs of doing so exceed the expected benefits. For instance, I haven't read and memorized the contents of my local phonebook because I rationally predict the return on investment would be negative. I haven't learned Icelandic for the same reason.

This theory explains why most Americans are mono-lingual, but most of the Dutch speak English. It explains why you cram before a test but forget the information afterward.

It also turns out—though it sounds paradoxical—that it can be rational to allow oneself to think in unrea-sonable ways. A person is said to be *rationally irrational* when they allow themselves to indulge in biased, unsci-entific, silly, or otherwise unreliable thought processes because the expected costs of overcoming bias exceed the expected benefits. In other words, it can be *instrumentally* rational (i.e., promote your goals or interests) to be *epis-temically* irrational (to think in unscientific, illogical, and unreasonable ways).

For instance, in the novel *1984*, IngSoc party elite O'Brien tortures the protagonist Winston. In order to demonstrate the party's total power, he wants to con-vince Winston to believe that 2 + 2 = 5. Once Winston accepts this and other absurdities, the torture will stop. In Winston's case, allowing himself to believe an absur-dity (2 + 2 = 5) serves his self-interest. In the same way, in medieval Europe, you'd have a strong incentive to believe Christianity, and in medieval and even the modern Middle East, to believe Islam, regardless of the truth of these reli-gions. In New England, you have a strong social incentive to love the Patriots and hate the Yankees. In contemporary political philosophy, given how much philosophers loves democracy, you have a social incentive to downplay or deny democracy's flaws and assert that the problems of democ-racy can be fixed with more democracy. Social rewards come to believers and social (and sometimes legal) punishments befall non-believers.

Most citizens do not invest in political knowledge because they find it boring and they realize their votes do not matter. The few who do invest in knowledge usually do so because they find politics interesting. But these citizens also turn out to be the most biased and tribalistic.[48] People are ignorant and irrational because democracy creates perverse incentives.

ON DEMOCRATIC LEGITIMACY

These findings cast doubt upon two major and closely related justifications for democratic government.

Many people believe that voting incentivizes politicians to perform well. The people vote for their interests. Politicians must cater to their interests in order to win power. Frequent elections help ensure that politicians respond to citizens' interests. Voting thus ensures that democracies have good performance.

On the contrary, people do not have a good sense of the general facts, what the problems are, what it takes to solve them, what the politicians want to do, and what they have in fact done. Elections are a poor mechanism for forcing politicians to serve citizens' interests, though they exert more pressure on politicians than the pressure dictators, absolute monarchs, or one-party states face.

A closely related view holds that democracy derives its legitimacy from the "consent" of the people, in the

48. Somin 2013; Mutz 2006.

non-literal sense that government does what the people say they want. More precisely, the theory holds that citizens have certain morally significant mental states—such as ontologies, theories, principles, preferences, desires, beliefs, attitudes, interests, worldviews, or whatnot—which in turn determine how they vote, which in turn determine the policies representatives will enact, and which constrain what representatives do. Call this the theory of "popular sovereignty."

Generally, defenders of the theory of popular sovereignty believe the legitimacy of our elected leaders, of our referenda, and so on, depend on two things:

1. That a sufficient number of citizens in a fair and free election voted for the winning outcome.
2. When citizens voted, their votes reflected their interests, beliefs, knowledge, and concerns.

Defenders of popular sovereignty hold that a sufficient number of citizens choosing to vote a certain way is a procedure that confers some degree of legitimacy and authority onto the winning political decision. It confers upon representatives the right to rule or upon referenda that force of law, within the limits set by the constitution and perhaps within certain external limits imposed by justice. They also think it matters that voters vote for the right kind of reasons. If voters were choosing at random, or choosing because they were completely misinformed, the moral significance of their choices would be greatly reduced.

However, it appears that in real-life democracy, all we can usually hope to get is 1, not 2. Voters' reasons for voting generally do not track sincere underlying interests, moral beliefs, or policy or outcome preferences.

For reasons like this, Achen and Bartels say that elections "turn out to be largely random events."[49] Far from being crucial junctures at which the will of the people is expressed, they are largely expensive ceremonies in which people express their fidelity to randomly allocated political tribes that have little to do with ideology, beliefs, or interests.

The will of the people? The people are ignorant, misinformed, irrational, tribalistic, and largely innocent of ideology. Their voting behavior does not much track their ideology (which they mostly lack) or their interests. Elections are largely random events.

So, what do we do about that?

49. Achen and Bartels 2016, 2.

Chapter 2

Is the Solution More Democracy?

IN *THE MYTH OF THE Rational Voter*, Bryan Caplan spends a few hundred pages demonstrating that the lay public holds systematically mistaken—and often stupid—beliefs about economic issues.[1] He does not expect democrats' faith to be shaken. Many pro-democracy philosophers and theorists are what he calls "democratic fundamentalists."[2] They reflexively claim that the solution to the problems of democracy is more democracy. Whenever a critic identifies a systematic problem with real-world democracy, they respond by saying the system is not *real* democracy.

This chapter rebuts the most intellectually serious versions of the "solution to the problems of democracy is more democracy" proposals. First, I'll respond to the idea that we merely need to educate voters better. Second, I'll examine the view that we can fix the problems of democracy by having citizens deliberate together in various ways. Third, I'll respond to arguments that hold that voters as a crowd are wise even if as individuals they are not.

1. Caplan 2007.
2. Caplan 2007.

Debating Democracy. Jason Brennan and Hélène Landemore, Oxford University Press. © Oxford University Press 2022. DOI: 10.1093/oso/9780197540817.003.0003

MORE EDUCATION?

One might think that the easy solution to voter ignorance is to provide more education. After all, the original justification for public education was to create a knowledgeable citizenry capable of self-rule.

Unfortunately, this response overestimates the effect of education on political knowledge. It misunderstands the perverse incentives that cause rational ignorance.

In fact, education has a weak independent effect on political knowledge. In the past sixty-five years, democratic populations worldwide have become more educated. The average number of years of schooling, the percentage of citizens who complete high school, and the percentage who attend college have risen significantly. The degree of political knowledge has remained flat.[3] People were badly educated and ignorant in 1958; today they are better educated but just as ignorant.

The Gallup polling company regularly gives voters a battery of thirty questions on basic political knowledge. As an independent variable, controlling for confounds, going from having a high school diploma to a bachelor's degree predicts that a person will get about one or two extra questions right.[4]

This makes sense when we remember the incentives democracy creates. People tend to be informed about something only if the expected benefits exceed the expected costs. They will tend to reason carefully only if the expected benefits exceed the expected costs.

3. Somin 2013.
4. Somin 2013.

We teach students much of what they need to vote well, but they allow themselves to forget that information. After all, individual votes make little difference, so it makes sense to remain ignorant of political knowledge. Most people who do invest in political knowledge do so because politics is a hobby, but then they are nearly always tribal players who indulge in their worst cognitive biases. Citizens tend to be either very ignorant and not very tribal, or somewhat better informed but very tribal and biased. That's what democracy has to work with.

DELIBERATIVE DEMOCRACY

Some ardent democrats would say everything in the previous chapter is beside the point because electoral democracy is a defective form of democracy. Instead, they argue that proper democracy has citizens *deliberate* with one another, not vote together.

"Deliberative democracy" refers to forms of democracy in which people come together to advance ideas, argue about those ideas, weigh pros and cons, listen to one another, and criticize each other's ideas with an open mind. Most deliberative democrats advocate an ideal under which citizens argue with one another in a dispassionate, scientific way, and then, as a result, reach a consensus about what ought to be done.

"Deliberation" connotes an orderly, reason-guided process. Theorist John Dryzek warns us that most political discussions do not quality as deliberation per se.[5] Rather,

5. Dryzek et al. 2019.

for something to count as deliberation, participants must follow certain norms of deliberation. For instance, Jürgen Habermas says deliberators should follow each of these rules:

1. Speakers must be consistent—they must not contradict themselves.
2. Speakers must treat like cases alike.
3. Speakers should use terms and language in a consistent way, to make sure they are all referring to the same things. (No equivocating or switching definitions in ways that would interfere with communication.)
4. Speakers must be sincere—they must assert only what they believe.
5. Speakers must provide reasons for introducing a subject or topic into the discussion.
6. Everyone who is competent to speak should be allowed into the discussion.
7. Speakers are to be allowed to discuss any topic, assert whatever they like, and express any needs—so long as they are sincere.
8. No one may coerce or manipulate another speaker.[6]

Of course, different deliberative democrats may have different standards for what counts as deliberation. But they agree that "deliberation" refers to a reason-guided process. Racist Uncle Joe and critical theory student Kate screaming over Thanksgiving dinner is not deliberation. Two political scientists carefully weighing the pros and

6. Habermas 2001.

cons of different ideas, comparing sources of evidence, and reaching consensus is deliberation.

Many deliberative democrats claim that deliberation will produce better political outcomes. They think getting citizens to deliberate together, especially if the citizens are selected at random and deliberation is overseen and curated by a trained moderator, will induce citizens to acquire more information, understand each other's points of view, think more carefully about politics, find common ground, and perhaps even reach a smart consensus on what to do.

We must avoid the "real democracy" problem here. It's easy to claim that *if* people follow Habermas's rules perfectly, then democratic deliberation will produce good results. The important institutional question is whether in the real world, if we try to get people to deliberate, they actually follow the rules of deliberation and produce good results.

By analogy, college fraternities aim to turn members into sophisticated, educated, honorable gentlemen who strive to promote the common good. Many fraternities undermine rather than support this goal. We can imagine a defender of fraternities saying, "Ah, but this just shows we need to find the optimal conditions for fraternity life. Fraternities have been problematic for the past 50 years, but they just aren't *doing it right*." This won't much impress the critic, since the point is that real people predictably won't behave the right way when they join fraternities. That they fail because they "don't do it the right way" is not an excuse but an explanation.

Similarly, it's easy to say that command economy socialism would be wonderful if only the central committee ran the economy exactly as political theorists want. From my armchair, I can easily imagine how the USSR could have created utopia on earth. But this provides no reason to advocate such institutions in the real world with real people. We need to know how they actually function.

The existing empirical work on democratic deliberation provides rather weak support for the supposed benefits deliberation is supposed to provide. For instance, in a comprehensive review of the empirical work on deliberative democracy, Tali Mendelberg finds:

- Deliberation sometimes facilitates cooperation among individuals in social dilemmas, but it undermines cooperation among groups. When people self-identify as members of a group, including as members of political groups, deliberation tend to make things worse, not better.[7] (Remember that in the real world people tend to self-identify as members of a political group.)
- When groups are of different sizes, deliberation tends to exacerbate conflict rather than mediate it.[8] (Note that in realistic circumstances, political groups tend to be different sizes.)
- Deliberation does tend to make people more aware of others' interests. However, other empirical work shows that if groups simply state their preferences *without* any discussion, this is just as effective as

7. Mendelberg 2002, 156.
8. Mendelberg 2002, 158.

stating their preferences *with* discussion.[9] So, *deliberation* per se isn't itself helpful in this case.

- Status-seeking drives much of the discussion. Instead of debating the facts, people try to win positions of influence and power over others.[10]
- Ideological minorities have disproportionate influence, and much of this influence can be attributed to groups' "social appeal."[11]
- High-status individuals talk more, are perceived as more accurate and credible, and have more influence, regardless of whether the high-status individuals actually know more.[12]
- During deliberation, people use language in biased and manipulative ways. For example, they switch between concrete and abstract language, in order to create the appearance that their side is essentially good (and any badness is accidental) while the other side is essentially bad (and any goodness is accidental). For example, if I describe my friend as kind, this abstract language suggests that she will regularly engage in kind behavior. If I say that my enemy donated some money to OxFam, this concrete language leaves open whether this kind of behavior matches my enemy's character and could be expected again.[13]
- Even when prodded by moderators to discuss controversial matters, groups tend to avoid conflict

9. Mendelberg 2002, 158.
10. Mendelberg 2002, 159.
11. Mendelberg 2002, 163–164.
12. Mendelberg 2002, 165–167.
13. Mendelberg 2002, 170–172.

and focus instead on mutually accepted beliefs and attitudes.[14]

- When a discussant mentions commonly held information or beliefs, this tends to make her seem smarter and more authoritative to others, and thus tends to increase her influence. Thus, Mendelberg concludes, "In most deliberations about public matters," group discussion tends to "amplify" intellectual biases rather than "neutralize" them.[15]

- Deliberation works best on "matters of objective truth"—when citizens are debating easily verifiable facts and statistics, such as information one could find on the US Census Bureau's website. "Other times"—when citizens debate morals, justice, or social scientific theories meant to evaluate those facts— "deliberation is likely to fail."[16]

That's from 2002. In a more recent survey of the literature, Mendelberg and C. Daniel Myers conclude with similar results.[17] There are some promising areas for further investigation, but a person who stands ready to declare that deliberation works is at best cherry-picking.

Other work finds similar negative results:

- Deliberation tends to move people toward more extreme versions of their ideologies rather than

---

14. Mendelberg 2002, 173.
15. Mendelberg 2002, 176, citing Kerr, MacCoun, and Kramer 1996.
16. Mendelberg 2002, 181.
17. C. Daniel Myers and Mendleberg 2013.

toward more moderate versions.[18] Legal theorist Cass Sunstein calls this the "Law of Group Polarization."

- Deliberation over sensitive matters—such as pornography laws—often leads to "hysteria" and "emotionalism," with parties to the debate feigning moral emergencies and booing and hissing at one another.[19]
- In actual deliberation, some groups get a greater voice than others, and leaders are often chosen in sexist or racially biased ways.[20]
- Deliberation often causes deliberators to choose positions inconsistent with their own views, positions which the deliberators "later regret."[21]
- Deliberation often causes deliberators to doubt there is a correct position at all—it leads to moral or political skepticism or nihilism.[22]
- Deliberation often makes citizens apathetic and agnostic about politics, and thus prevents them from participating or acting. Exposure to contrary points of view tends to induce citizens to disengage with politics—it reduces their degree of civic participation.[23]

18. Sunstein 2002.
19. Downs 1989.
20. Ellsworth 1989, 213; Cohen 1982, 210–211; Marsden 1987, 63–64.
21. Ryfe 2005, 54.
22. Ryfe 2005, 54.
23. See Mutz 2006.

- During deliberation, citizens often change their preferences and reach consensus only because they are manipulated by powerful special interests.[24]
- Consensus often occurs only because citizens purposefully avoid controversial topics, even during organized deliberative forums designed to make them confront those topics.[25]
- Rather than causing consensus, public deliberation might cause disagreement and the formation of in-groups and out-groups.[26] It can even lead to violence.[27]
- Citizens prefer *not* to engage in deliberative modes of reasoning, and they prefer that deliberation not last very long.[28] They dislike deliberating.

Now, some work finds some positive results. Deliberative democrats of course seize on this work and think the critical work is misguided. They accuse people who think deliberation doesn't work of cherry-picking the research, though oddly, by "cherry-picking" they seem to be mean summarizing the majority of the work. In a recent review of the literature, Nicole Curato, John Dryzek, Selen Ercan, Carolyn Hendriks, and Simon Neimeyer say:

> Political theorist David Miller and, later, John Dryzek and political philosopher Christian List have demonstrated formally that deliberation can, among other responses:

---

24. See Stokes 1998.
25. Hibbing and Theiss-Morse 2002.
26. See Hibbing and Theiss-Morse 2002.
27. Mutz 2006, 89.
28. Somin 2013, 53.

1) induce agreement to restrict the ability of actors to introduce new options that destabilize the decision process and
2) structure the preferences of participants such that they
become "single-peaked" along one dimension, thus reducing
the prevalence of manipulable cycles across alternatives
(in which option A beats B in a majority vote, B beats C, and
C beats A). Empirical research confirms this effect.[29]

Oddly, this is the only major positive empirical result they
list. They respond to Mendelberg's list of the pathologies of
deliberation by saying that "Resolution here requires distin-
guishing carefully between deliberation and discussion."[30]
This sounds like the "college fraternities aren't doing it right"
or "The USSR wasn't real socialism" defense. Of course, if
people behaved exactly the way the theorists wanted, good
things will happen, but what we need to know when we
implement rules is how people will actually behave.

IMPLEMENTING DELIBERATIVE DEMOCRACY IN THE REAL WORLD

Bruce Ackerman and James Fishkin suggest that we create a national holiday called "Deliberation Day." Citizens
receive a paid day off, but are required to attend moder-
ated, local political discussions.[31] The hope is that citizens
will be better informed and more enlightened when the
general election comes.

29. Curato et al. 2017.
30. Curato et al. 2017.
31. Ackerman and Fishkin 2005.

Others advocate more radical ideas: Instead of having a straight election or a referendum, we could have a "deliberative poll." Five hundred citizens will be selected at random, much like jurors are selected for jury duty. They will be compensated but forced to attend, say, a weekend or week-long workshop where they will read relevant material and engage in deliberation overseen by a trained government moderator. They will be asked to reach a decision, which will be implemented into law. Instead of having citizens choose leaders to craft law, we will recruit citizens to create law directly. Since democracy is the rule of the people, why not have the people rule?

In response to these proposals, legal theorist Ilya Somin, author of *Democracy and Political Ignorance*, offers a number of serious objections. First, it is implausible that in one day or even over a few weeks, citizens will be able to cover and understand even a tiny portion of the issues they need to understand. Deliberation Day's deliberations last eight hours. That won't cut it.

Second, even if citizens focus narrowly on one problem, it often takes years of specialized training to understand even a small aspect of that one problem. For instance, on the issue of international trade, even taking a semester of economics is not enough to ensure people know all the pertinent information, theory, and trade-offs. The world's smartest people can spend their entire lives researching one major issue (and deliberating with other such researchers) and not be sure what to do, so it's absurd to think average people could figure it out in three days, or three months, or even a year.

Third, and perhaps the most fatal worry, is this:

> Incumbent political leaders would have to enact [Deliberation
> Day or a deliberative poll]. In particular, they would have
> to determine the methods for selecting the issues to be dis-
> cussed and the spokespersons for the opposing parties. This
> process would create numerous opportunities for manipula-
> tion. For instance, if the Republicans have control of Congress
> when the Deliberation Day bill is passed, they could try to
> focus the process on issues where they know the Republican
> Party would have an edge. Similarly, the parties and their
> spokespeople could use the process to appeal to voters' ratio-
> nal irrationality, competing with each other in reinforcing the
> citizens' pre-existing biases rather than genuinely informing
> them. Such manipulations were unlikely to be as serious a
> problem in Fishkin's and his colleagues' previous poll experi-
> ments, when the political stakes were not so high.[32]

It's difficult to get deliberation to work well in laboratory or experimental conditions, when nothing is at stake.
But what will happen in the real world when a great deal is at
stake? If, like most people, you think the politicians on the
other side are corrupt and stupid, what will happen when
your stupid and corrupt enemies run Deliberation Day?

In some of her related recent work, Landemore extols
the virtues of internet-based crowdsourcing, an alternative to the more organized forms of deliberation. She uses
Iceland's experiment with crowdsourcing constitutional
changes as a case study.[33]

Iceland benefits from factors that make democratic
deliberation and consensus relatively easy to achieve: it

32. Somin 2013, 179–180.
33. Landemore 2017.

is small, ethnically homogenous, and highly educated; it has low levels of political polarization,[34] very high rates of human development, high rates of interpersonal trust among its citizens, and a strong history of civic involvement, broadly understood. Iceland should be able to make open democracy succeed if anyone can. But if they can, this does not mean larger, less homogenous countries such as France could easily copy their example.

Landemore describes a situation in which "seven government experts" were asked to suggest revisions to the Icelandic constitution's provision on religious freedom. In turn, twenty-five lay citizens were also asked to propose a revision, which they partially crowd-sourced through the internet. In the end, the crowd-sourced proposal was, both Landemore and I agree, superior to the "expert" version, mostly because it included somewhat more inclusive language and left a little less discretion to parliament.

Landemore sees this as evidence that in a kind of open democracy, with less structured deliberation, the uneducated many can and will outperform the expert few. I'm unconvinced. I am in general suspicious of extrapolating general principles from individual case studies. This borders on anecdotal reasoning. But my bigger worry is that the laypeople were given a relatively easy task. They weren't being asked to write fine policy details on a hard question, such as what the optimal way to regulate diesel emissions is, or exactly how Iceland should participate in the NATO alliance in the face of Russia's newfound aggression. They were instead asked to write a meta-legal principle on

34. Önnudóttir and Harðarson 2018.

freedom of religion for a constitution. They have hundreds of years of history and thousands of legal case studies from hundreds of different constitutions upon which to draw. They could have examined at great length how different religious freedom provisions in different constitutions have tended to work. They could have, if they wanted, copied the language from already existing, well-functioning constitutions written by experts.

Despite all these advantages, the text the laypeople produced strikes me as obviously worse than the religion freedom provisions (written by legislators or experts) in the constitutions of many other liberal countries. They couldn't manage to de-establish the state Lutheran church in a country with extremely high rates of atheism and low rates of religious observance. Landemore discusses at some length why de-establishment was not a live option—many citizens wish to maintain the state church they do not attend. But that seems like a poor excuse, not a justification. Iceland's performance here was bad and they should feel bad.

MIRACLES OF AGGREGATION: ARE CROWDS WISE?

Some defend democracy by extolling the wisdom of crowds. Under certain circumstances, large crowds of people can be reliable even though the individuals within those crowds are not.

For instance, consider the familiar game of guessing the number of jellybeans in a jar. Most make bad guesses. But when we average people's guesses together, the mean guess becomes more accurate. The more people, the more accurate the mean guess.

Some theorists say voting is like that. Any individual voter might be ignorant and misinformed, but perhaps "averaging" or aggregating their votes provides an accurate result.

One simple argument for this idea is called the Miracle of Aggregation. Suppose there are two candidates, Good and Awful. Suppose all the well-informed voters recognize Good is better than Awful, and so vote for Good. Suppose the well-informed voters make up only 2% of the electorate. The other 98% are completely, totally ignorant. One might think that ignorant voters will have no basis to prefer Good to Awful or Awful to Good, and so they will vote randomly. It will be like they flip a coin. So long as there are lots of ignorant voters, then half will vote for Good and half for Awful. Since Good gets all the informed voters' votes, she wins the majority and carries the election. Thus, the argument goes, a very large electorate made up almost entirely of uninformed voters will perform as well as a well-informed electorate.

Another closely related idea is known as Condorcet's Jury Theorem. This theorem holds that (1) if a group is making a decision, and (2) the average reliability of individual group members is greater than chance, then (3) as the size of the group gets larger, the (4) probability that the group will select the right answer approaches 1. Note, however, that this theorem also says that if the average reliability of the group is less than chance, the probability that the group will select the right answer approaches 0 (i.e., the probability they will select the wrong answer approaches 1).

A final theorem often cited in support of democracy is the Hong–Page Theorem. What precisely this theorem means in the abstract, and what it means for democracy, is disputed. I'll spend more time discussing it below. However, a friendly description of it is that under the right conditions, cognitive diversity among the participants in a collective decision-making process better contributes to that process producing right outcomes than increasing the participants' individual reliability or ability.[35] This is often summarized as saying that "cognitive diversity trumps ability."

The Hong–Page Theorem is subject to considerably more controversy than the other two theorems. Mathematician Abigail Thompson claims that the proof of the Hong–Page Theorem fails, as it rests on several identifiable mathematical errors. She further claims that the theorem has trivial content, because it assumes what it intends to prove, because the mathematical stand-in for "diversity" in the theorem does not correspond to anything that we would call "cognitive diversity" in the real world, and because the proof is not generalizable.[36] Similarly, Paul Quirk, among others, claims that the "proof" depends upon a series of computer experiments "strongly biased toward that result [that diversity trumps ability] and argues that it tells us nothing about decision-making in real-world political settings."[37] Further, some complain, the reason why "diversity trumps ability" in the Hong–Page Theorem is that the theorem in effect models large groups as including the

35. Page and Hong 2004.
36. Thompson 2014.
37. Quirk 2014.

most elite performers and deferring to them when they are right. Philosopher David Wallace argues that the theorem assumes what it is supposed to prove, that is, that "(1) when a group of agents all have the same skill-set, it doesn't matter how many of them there are—they can't do better than a single agent with that skill-set; and (2) whenever some group of agents gets stuck, there'll always be an agent with a different skill-set who can help them out." The theorem is supposed to prove this, he says, but in fact Hong and Page bake these into their *premises*. Thus, their result is trivial.[38]

I won't dwell on these issues here because they are deeply technical. (Later in this book, in my response to Landemore's half, I will get into the technical issues. I will argue that proof of the Hong-Page Theorem turns out to be trivial and question-begging, and that it does not really show that diversity trumps ability. Since her defense of democracy rests on the theorem, I will argue her defense cannot succeed.) For now, I will instead grant that the theorem means what its defenders think it means, but then argue even then it cannot be used to defend democracy.

Each of these theorems offers a mathematical model under which groups as a whole might be highly reliable even though none or few of the participants within the group are. They each state that if certain conditions are met, then collective decision procedures will produce smart outcomes.

However, these kinds of aggregative phenomena occur only when errors tend to be symmetrically distributed and

38. https://leiterreports.typepad.com/blog/2019/11/a-mathematical-proof-that-diversity-trumps-ability-turns-out-to-be-just-more-diversity-blather.html

so tend to cancel each other out.[39] If one can show that errors are not randomly or symmetrically distributed or, more broadly, that citizens tend to make systematic mistakes, tend to follow one another's opinions, or tend to be systematically misinformed and unreliable, then these mathematical theorems cannot be used in support of democracy.

In the previous chapter, I discussed the empirical work on voter behavior and psychology, This literature says:

1. Citizens do not form their ideas independently and separately. Instead, they follow one another, and in particular, tend to parrot whatever their party happens to say.
2. Citizens vote for largely non-cognitive and non-ideological problems. They are cheering for their team, not trying to discover the right answer.
3. Most citizens have very unsophisticated mental models of politics and very low levels of information.
4. Citizens make systematic errors and are systematically mistaken about a wide range of basic political facts and more advanced social scientific knowledge.

I do not see how one can dispute these facts. The degree of reasonable disagreement is about whether these problems are between moderately to very severe. But together they are fatal to aggregative defenses of democracy.

---

39. Landemore 2012, 195.

Further, even though a large percentage of voters cannot identify the incumbent candidates, nevertheless, voters persistently tend to vote for the incumbents against challengers. On this point, Ilya Somin notes that incumbent bias alone has been shown to defeat the Miracle of Aggregation:

> A recent attempt to test the [Miracle of Aggregation] on samples drawn from six recent presidential elections (1972–1992) found that, controlling for various background characteristics of voters, poor information produces an average aggregate bias of 5 percent in favor of the incumbent.[40]

Much of Landemore's work defending democracy makes heavy use of the Hong–Page Theorem. She summarizes her thesis: "For most political problems, and under conditions conducive to proper deliberation and proper use of majority rule, a democratic procedure is likely to be a better decision procedure than any nondemocratic procedure, such as a council of experts or a benevolent dictator."[41] Above, I mentioned that whether the theorem has been proven, whether it is trivial, whether it is generalizable, and whether the concept of "diversity" tracks anything in the theorem are hotly contested. (Again, in my response to Landemore later in this book, I will debunk the Hong–Page Theorem.)

For the sake of argument, let's grant that the Hong–Page Theorem is correct, and that it says what Hong, Page,

---

40. Somin 1998, 431. For empirical confirmation of these claims, see Bartels 1996; Alvarez 1997.
41. Landemore 2012, 3.

and Landemore think it says. What does it say? Page himself clarifies: The Hong–Page Theorem says that under the right conditions, cognitive diversity among the participants in a collective decision-making process better contributes to that process producing right outcomes than increasing the participants' individual reliability or ability. These conditions include: (1) the participants must have genuinely diverse models of the world, (2) the participants must have sufficiently complex models of the world, (3) the participants must agree on what the problem is and what would count as a solution, (4) the participants must all be trying to solve the problem together, and (5) the participants must be willing to learn from others and take advantage of other participants' knowledge.[42]

My worry is that in real-world elections, real-world "deliberation" (or "discussion," if you prefer) and other real-world democratic contexts, these conditions are almost never met. In fact, citizens lack much cognitive diversity. They parrot the ideas of their team and post-hoc rationalize that they agree with their party's platform. Their beliefs tend to cluster together (e.g., they believe climate change is real and anthropogenic if and only if they also advocate increased gun control and if and only if they are pro-choice). Our errors do not cancel each other out but compound, because we make systematic mistakes. In fact, most citizens have almost entirely unsophisticated mental models of the problems they wish to solve. Many citizens come forth with no knowledge or models at all. In fact, when we deliberate or vote, we rarely agree on what

---

42. Somin 2013, 114; Hong and Page 2004, 163–186.

the problems are and what would count, in the abstract, as solutions. In fact, we are not trying to solve problems together. In fact, we are not willing to learn from or take advantage of others' knowledge. Instead, we suffer from confirmation bias and disconfirmation bias, so we dismiss others' ideas and evidence and react by becoming more strongly entrenched in our own.

Chapter 3

Democracy: Maybe Less Is More

DEMOCRACY IS THE RULE OF the people, but it incentivizes them to be ignorant, misinformed, tribalistic, bad at deliberating, and bad at processing information. They are mostly innocent of ideology and political belief, and what beliefs they have usually arise from conformity to their party rather than from due consideration of their real interests. We have little reason to believe that wisdom is an emergent feature of the crowd.

In this chapter, I will argue that one solution to the problems of democracy is . . . less democracy. Perhaps the solution is not merely less democracy, but less politics, period.

That is, even if we retain what is overall a democratic form of government, the problems of political ignorance, misinformation, bias, and tribalism explain why it's a good idea to keep certain issues away from voters. One reason democratic governments around the world perform as well as they do is that they are not completely democratic. In other cases, the solution is to keep matters away from political control altogether.

Debating Democracy. Jason Brennan and Hélène Landemore, Oxford University Press. © Oxford University Press 2022. DOI: 10.1093/oso/9780197540817.003.0004

EPISTEMIC THEORIES
OF DEMOCRACY

Epistemic or instrumentalist theories of democracy hold that part of what justifies democratic political structures over alternative institutions is that democracy has a sufficiently strong tendency to make correct political decisions, as judged by procedure-independent standards.[1] Landemore's defense of democracy is epistemic/instrumentalist so defined.

Epistemic democrats and their intellectual opponents tend to focus on whether fundamental political power, and the basic *form* of government, should be democratic or something else.[2] I worry that this debate tends to oversimplify things and ignore some important questions, which any epistemic theory must answer:

1. Which issues are subject to political decision-making, at all, as a matter of normal course and as a matter of reserve powers?
2. Even if a society should be fundamentally democratic, should certain political decisions be made through alternative, non-democratic methods, subject to democratic checks?

1. Schwartzberg 2015.
2. An epistocracy is a political system which, by law, in some way apportions fundamental political power according to some legal criterion of knowledge, expertise, or political competence.

The first question concerns what we might call the scope of politics; the second concerns the scope of democracy.

Not everything should be subject to political decision-making. Some issues properly remain outside the sphere of politics, either as a matter of normal course or even in principle. So far, though, epistemic democrats remain mostly silent about what properly goes inside or outside the sphere of political decision-making.

Whether something is properly subject to political control is at least in part determined by epistemic considerations. For instance, if for a given issue, *all* forms of political decision-making are inferior to non-political methods, then that issue should stay outside the scope (at least presumptively) of politics. Epistemic democrats such as Landemore should—in light of their own commitments—accept this very conclusion.

THE EPISTEMIC SELECTION PRINCIPLE

Every epistemic or instrumentalist theory of politics contains some version of what I'll call the *Epistemic Selection Principle*:

Epistemic Selection Principle
Choose the institutional framework that tends to produce the best decisions or deliver the best results, where the results are judged by the correct procedure-independent standards, whatever those are.

Different epistemic theories contain different variations on this principle. What unites epistemic theories is that they give some version of this principle significant weight. The greater the weight or the stronger the version of the principle, the more epistemic the theory is.

THE RIGHT TO COMPETENT GOVERNANCE

I think everyone—not just philosophers already committed to judging democracy by its results—must take epistemic considerations seriously. Upon reflection, we'll see that most of us already have strong moral intuitions in favor of the idea that the legitimacy and authority of government depend in significant part on its competence and reliability.

To illustrate, consider an analogy. Imagine a defendant has been accused of first-degree murder. During the trial, both the prosecution and defense call witnesses, present evidence, challenge arguments, and the like. Afterward, the jury retires to deliberate about whether the defendant is guilty. Suppose after a few hours, they come forth and declare him guilty. However, suppose we also learn the jury had any of the following features:

1. *Ignorance.* The jury paid no attention to the facts of the case, slept through the trial, and did not read the transcript. They found him guilty by flipping a coin.
2. *Misinformation.* The jury deeply misunderstood the facts of the case. For instance, they had clearly false

beliefs about where the defendant was during the murder, what the defendant's relationship to the victim was, and so on. Their false beliefs explain why they found him guilty.

3. *Tribalism.* It turns out the jurors were "vote guilty" kinds of people. That is, they each had a weird quirk where they always voted guilty, regardless of the evidence, because that's what their neighbors and friends tended to do. If we gave them hundred trials, they'd say guilty every time, regardless of the evidence.

4. *Malice.* The jurors found the defendant guilty because they didn't like his race, sex, gender, sexual orientation, job, birthplace, or some other irrelevant factor.

5. *Selfishness/Conflict of Interest/Corruption.* They found guilty because they took a bribe.

6. *Irrationality.* The jurors found the defendant guilty because they processed information in deeply irrational ways.

7. *Stupidity/Incompetence:* The jurors found the defendant guilty because they lacked the capacity to understand the information they were presented.

If we learned the jurors acted in any combination of these ways, we would think it's a miscarriage of justice to enforce their decision. The jurors owe it to society, as our representatives, and to the defendant as well, to conduct a fair, impartial, unbiased trail, and to reason in truth-conductive, reliable ways. In this case, we would conclude the jury's decision should be thrown out and the trial conducted again.

The jury's decision is high stakes. They have the power to deprive a person of liberty and possibly his life. Their decision will be imposed involuntarily upon the defendant. Further, they are charged with administering justice. In cases like this, it seems plausible that the jury is obligated to make their decision competently and in good faith. Moreover, it is permissible to enforce their decision only if they make it competently and in good faith.

That seems true not merely of a jury decision, but of many other political decisions. Many decisions are high stakes. They can greatly affect other people's welfare, alter their life prospects, and deprive them of life, liberty, property, and happiness. The people making these decisions are usually charged with acting on behalf of the common good and are supposed to aim for just outcomes. Thus, I think juries, judges, police officers, presidents, legislators, bureaucrats, governors, and even *the voting public* are constrained by what I call the *Competence Principle*:

> It is presumed to be unjust and to violate a citizen's rights to forcibly deprive them of life, liberty, or property, or significantly harm their life prospects, as a result of decisions made by an incompetent deliberative body, or as a result of decisions made in an incompetent way or in bad faith. Political decisions are presumed legitimate and authoritative only when produced by competent political bodies in a competent way and in good faith.

The idea here is that high-stakes decisions, imposed and enforced through violence, must be made by a competent body in a competent way, acting in good faith. If they are not, the decisions are presumed illegitimate.

But let me put this more bluntly and in less legalistic language. Exercising political power over others is a big deal. You can deeply harm them, deprive them of their rights, and even kill them. If you are going to exercise power, you better do so in good faith and know what you are doing. I take that to be a bare minimal condition of your right to rule. Anything less than that is, frankly, evil.

I realize "evil" is a dramatic word, but it's the right word. If a jury sends you to jail without carefully thinking through the evidence, that's evil. If a president sends you to war because it helps his stocks, that's evil. The only reason to put up with incompetent exercises of power is if we are forced by circumstances to do so, and we cannot find any competent mechanism to make decisions.

If defendants can demand competence from juries, can citizens also demand competence from the electorate? Notice that the electorate's decisions have the same morally salient features as the decisions of juries:

1. Electorates are charged with making morally momentous decisions, as they must decide how to apply principles of justice, and how to shape many of the basic institutions of society. They are one of the main vehicles through which justice is to be established.

2. Electoral decisions tend to be of major significance. They can significantly alter the life prospects of citizens, and deprive them of life, liberty, and property.

3. The electorate claims sole jurisdiction for making certain kinds of decisions over certain people

within a geographic area. The electorate expects people to accept and abide by their decisions.

4. The outcomes of decisions are imposed involuntarily through violence and threats of violence.

Combined, these are grounds for holding that the Competence Principle applies not merely to juries, but to the electorate as a whole. The relationship of the electorate to the governed is morally similar to the relationship between jurists and a defendant. The grounds for holding the jury must act competently and in good faith apply to the electorate as well.

Of course, these relationships are not perfectly analogous. On one hand, compared to typical defendants, typical citizens have stronger grounds for demanding competence. Many defendants are in fact guilty and have in fact forfeited some of their rights. The defendants know that some of their rights have been forfeited. For them to demand competence is just to demand that juries take care in determining what the defendants already know. In contrast, most citizens are innocent and have forfeited none of their rights. They retain the strong liberal presumption against interference of any kind. They retain the strong presumption that evils not be visited upon them by force. Thus, the average citizen is in a stronger position than the average defendant to demand competence.

On the other hand, there is some sense in which the electorate is exercising power over itself, while the jury is exercising power over someone else. But it is not as though all people unanimously agree to political outcomes. Rather, some proper subset of the people gets its way, and can impose its way upon all the other people, including losing voters, innocent resident aliens, children, and non-voters. If the majority incompetently choose the warmongering presidents, it's not merely that majority who suffer the consequences of their incompetence.

I won't offer a precise theory of what constitutes competence and what doesn't. Any theory is bound to be controversial, and I don't need to resolve that controversy for my argument to go through. Consider, by analogy, an electorate behaving like the bad juries above. We ask the electorate to pick the US president, a person who has tremendous unchecked political power, including the power (and tendency) to make war and to kill foreigners and foreign leaders almost at will. Now suppose the electorate picks a candidate, but does so in ignorance, because of misinformation, out of malice, due to perverse tribalism, out of objectionable selfishness within a conflict of interest, or from serious cognitive bias and deficiencies in reasoning. There is no plausible theory that holds these are competent, reliable, or good-faith decision mechanisms. As we saw in chapter 1, most voters fall far below any reasonable cut-off for the boundary between competent and incompetent.

DO ELECTIONS MATTER?

A stronger objection to my argument here is to say that elections do not matter that much and so do not qualify as "high-stakes" in the appropriate sense. There is certainly some truth to this. For instance, in a recent paper, political scientists Adam Dynes and John Holbein carefully and rigorously measure how parties affect economic, education, crime, family, social, environmental, and health outcomes. They find zero difference between Republican and Democratic state governments over any short-term measurable period.[3]

Now, I don't take that quite to show that elections don't matter so much as to show the two long-term ruling parties perform about the same. However, presumably electing the Libertarians or the Communist Party would have a stronger effect. Further, there is still significant evidence that Republicans and Democrats tend to push candidates in the middle of the ideological spectrum of the voters in a given region—though there is also strong evidence that causation also goes the other way. If so, then the quality of the candidates depends in significant part on the quality of the voters.

Rather than try to definitively answer the question of how much elections matter, I'll pose the issue in the form of a dilemma for the other side. Either you hold elections matter, in terms of their impact on policy or outcomes, or you don't. Of course, you can debate how much they matter. You can assign a number from, say, one to one hundred on how much impact you think voters have through elections.

If you think elections do matter and are high stakes, then the argument over the past two chapters should disturb you. Voters routinely violate the Competence Principle. We ask voters to choose leaders and, in some cases, to vote directly on policy, but voters are mostly ignorant, misinformed, and irrational; they choose sides for capricious reasons and reason about politics in ways we would recognize as infantile in any other sphere of life; they do not

3. Dynes and Holbein 2019.

vote on the basis of ideology or their interests; they attach themselves to parties for essentially arbitrary reasons.

If you think elections don't matter at all or matter very little, then they aren't subject to the Competence Principle because they are not sufficiently high stakes. This means that voters' psychology does not matter because their votes as a whole do not matter, and their votes do not matter because elections do not matter.

But now, having said that, you must swallow some big bullets. If elections do not affect policy outcomes in a significant way, then it's hard to see why one would think democracy is justified. Why would it matter if everyone gets to vote, or if they get to vote equally? Why not, say, disenfranchise all women, since, by hypothesis, elections do not matter and do affect outcomes?

If elections do not significantly affect outcomes, then presumably you would be indifferent to me (1) waving a magic wand that makes everyone perfectly informed, (2) maintaining the status quo, or (3) waving a magic wand that makes everyone advocate, say, fascism or Leninism. Presumably you are in favor of eliminating all civics education, since by hypothesis, elections don't matter and so having an educated citizenry does not matter. If elections don't matter, then presumably we should dispense with them entirely, or hold them once a generation. And so on.

In my experience, no one is willing to bite these bullets. "Elections don't matter that much" is used as an objection to my argument but the objector never means it.

As an aside, I am often accused of defending an elitist view of democracy. But notice that my *premises* are not elitist. I have never argued that smart people ought to rule because they are smarter, or that intelligence and knowledge entitles you to power. (Indeed, I am skeptical than anyone should have power over anyone else, period.) Rather, I am making what I take as a bland, theory-neutral point: When you exercise significant power over others, you owe it to them to do so competently and in good faith. This is not a liberal, libertarian, conservative, or socialist idea. Rather, it's an idea that can and I think must be fit into any political theory. I am simply asking that we hold everyone who exercises significant power over others to basic and rather *low* moral standards. I don't regard voters as somehow, through moral magic, exempt from these low moral standards. Unfortunately, we have strong evidence that voters systematically fail to meet them.

HOW TO APPLY THESE PRINCIPLES: THE OPTIONS

The Epistemic Selection Principle tells us to choose the institutional framework that is likely to produce the most just or overall best results, as judged by independent standards. Landemore is committed to it.

The Competence Principle is an independent idea. Rather than holding that we should pick the best-functioning institutional framework, it tells us that high-stakes political decisions are illegitimate when made incompetently or in bad faith. It tells us to *avoid* imbuing incompetent or bad-faith bodies with power. It tells us that a person or group should have power over a given issue *only if* they will use it competently and in good faith.

Both principles give us many options about what to do, though. Complying with them could require paying attention to and altering any of the following aspects of political decision-making:

1. *Scale*: The number of people or geographic range over which a particular decision, law, or policy applies.
2. *Timing*: How quickly or slowly decisions are made, or when the decisions are made.
3. *Form*: Who rules and how power is distributed among the people who rule.
4. *Scope*: Which issues and topics are regularly or in principle subjected to political decision-making.

Existing debates about the epistemic credentials of democracy largely focus merely on the question of the overall *form* of government, such as whether governments should be democratic. Again, this oversimplifies the debate about epistemic merits of democracy. If we want to make government perform better, or eliminate the most incompetent and unreliable decision-making methods, we have plenty of options.

The *scale* of government—or other institutions— concerns the number of people or the geographic range over which a particular decision is made or over which some political body holds power. Consider, for instance, that the size of many counties or similar political units around the world were chosen on the basis of available technology. The sheriff should have jurisdiction over an area that could be covered in one-day's horse ride. It may turn out that more localized, federalized, and devolved forms of government function better than more centralized governments, or it may not. In addition, there are debates about whether ethnic and linguistic diversity undermine interpersonal trust and as a result impede political functioning.[4] Communist-style property institutions seem to function well on a small scale, for instance, among the one-hundred-person or fewer Hutterite colonies, but not on a large scale among diverse strangers.[5]

The *timing* of government concerns when and how quickly political decisions are made. For instance, it may turn out as empirical matter, that certain decisions tend to be more reliable if made after a "cooling-off" period. Political theorist Greg Weiner argues that this was James Madison's intention in designing the US Constitution—the goal was not so much to put in checks and balances to reduce majoritarian tyranny or factionalism, but instead to reduce hot-headed responses to problems.[6] Or, consider the famous and disturbing study that finds that whether judges in parole hearings decide to grant parole or not seems to be overwhelmingly determined by how recently the judges have had a break and a snack.[7] If such results hold up, this tells us that parole hearings should not be scheduled back to back, because having tired and hungry judges causes them to make unjust decisions.

The *form* of government concerns which people are granted power and in what proportion. In an absolute monarchy or dictatorship, one person holds all the fundamental power. In an aristocracy or oligarchy, a small group of elites share the fundamental power, while most

4. Alesina, Spolaore, and Wacziarg 2005.
5. Schmidtz 1994.
6. Weiner 2012.
7. Danzinger, Levav, and Avniam-Pesso 2011.

are excluded. In a democracy, each person is entitled to an equal share of fundamental power. In practice, though, no kingdoms are truly absolute (power is always shared by others) and no democracies are truly equal (some people always have more effective power than others).

Further, the form of government concerns specific questions about how decisions are made. Is there a strong central government or is power devolved? Is there a multi-cameral or unicameral legislature? Is there a strong or weak executive? What kind of oversight do courts have over legislation? Which voting system does the government use, if any? Are legislators elected, appointed, or chosen by lottery? If we care about how well government performs, we should not simply ask whether the government should be democratic, but also ask which kinds of democracies perform the best. Perhaps parliamentary systems with weak executives and proportional voting outperform, say, the American system.

The *scope* of government concerns which issues are subject to political decision-making, either as a matter of normal course or as a matter of reserve powers in unusual or emergency decision-making. While the form of government is about *who* has power, the scope concerns over *what* they have power.

For instance, almost no one thinks governments should decide which consenting adults may marry one another, beyond restrictions preventing incest. The reason for rejecting the subjection of such decisions to political choice is not simply that it would violate citizens' autonomous rights, but also because a Ministry of Marriage would not make good decisions.

Similarly, modern economics holds that governments are generally incompetent to set prices for goods and services or to engage in widespread central planning of the economy. If contemporary economics is correct, then, the principle of epistemic selection tells us to leave a great deal of fundamental economic planning outside the scope of government, whatever form the government may otherwise have. Further, to what degree governments can effectively intervene or regulate the economy on the margins is itself largely an empirical question, which depends in part on how badly such regulation will be subject to rent-seeking or other forms of government failure. It is something a democratic vote might *discover*, but not quite something it can just *decide*. Again, the principle of epistemic selection and the Competence Principle tell us to set the scope of political regulation of markets in part by determining how well political regulation works. The less competent government is, or the less it acts in good faith, the less right it has to regulate and the less power it may have.

Linguists make the same conclusion about language. Norms of language, including changes in vocabulary, pronunciation, or grammar, arise spontaneously, through the interactions of speakers over time, without any central directing agency. Planned languages, such as Esperanto, do not catch on. While government boards can influence language here and there, and in some cases help improve alphabets, in general, no one thinks governments to be competent to create and plan our languages. Similar remarks apply to many other social norms or institutions. One reason we might reject having government set the rules of fashion or religion is that government bureaucracies would do so less competently than civil society.

Consider another example: When David Estlund analyzes why democracy is preferable to anarchy, he confines himself to discussing the issue of punishment.[8] He does not offer any general proof. He has readers imagine a cartoon society called Anarchic Prejuria.[9] In Prejuria, there are widely recognized moral and social norms, and people largely agree upon the content of justice. However, there are no institutions for enforcing the rules of justice or for apprehending, trying, or punishing offenders. Instead, every individual engages in private punishment. Estlund thinks this would lead to a humanitarian disaster, while a democratic state with jury system would greatly outperform it.[10]

Two problems are immediately noticeable with this argument. First, it's a strawman critique of anarchism; no anarchist could regard Estlund as providing plausible characterization of their view. Instead, both left and right anarchists have described at length how various non-state mechanisms of enforcement might function, and they have argued at length that such mechanisms might outperform state-based systems.[11] Whether these institutions are workable is not our concern. I merely note here that Estlund ignores this anarchist literature. He loads the intellectual dice in his favor by assuming that anarchism means ad hoc, private enforcement, while anarchism

---

8. Estlund 2007, 146.
9. Estlund 2007, 138.
10. Estlund 2007, 145–147.
11. E.g., see Huemer 2013; Leeson 2016; Stringham 2014; Ostrom 1990.

should instead be regarded as having various non-state institutional mechanisms of enforcement.

The second problem is that even if the argument for government criminal justice over anarchic enforcement goes through, that hardly tells us about *other* issues. On the price of commodities, anarchic methods (i.e., market forces of supply and demand) beat democratic methods (e.g., setting prices through deliberation). The question is not, Estlund would agree, whether everything should be decided through democratic mechanisms or some other mechanism, but instead, for all possible institutions, which mechanism would produce the best results. Even if Estlund has strong grounds for arguing that fundamental political power should be democratic, that leaves open which decisions should be subject to political control and which should be decided by social norms, civil society, and/ or markets.

The issue is not whether we should have everything subject to some form of democratic control, everything decided through random selection, or everything decided by whatever exists of civil society, private choices, or markets, devoid of government. Rather, this should be determined on a case-by-case or issue-by-issue basis. Even if government is democratic, many issues should remain largely outside the scope of that government's control.

10% LESS DEMOCRACY

In the recent, remarkable book *10% Less Democracy*, Garrett Jones splashes some cold water on democracy's most excited enthusiasts. Jones's major point is that if we examine the relationship between (A) how democratic a country is and (B) various desirable outcomes, such as prosperity, growth, stability, and so on, we do not see a simple positive relationship. Rather, it's an upside-down U-shaped curve. Too little democracy is a bad thing, but so is too much democracy. The US, France, and many other countries are on many issues on the right side of the curve; that is, they will generate better outcomes if they scale back a bit. Democracy is good, but only in moderation.

Much of what Jones does is review the existing empirical work in economics to show there is more or less a consensus on each of the following cases where *less* democracy produces better outcomes[12]:

1. Longer term limits and longer terms for representatives produce better outcomes. When politicians have short careers and short terms, they not only spend too much of their time campaigning (and, in the US, fundraising), but they also pursue short-term goals at the expense of long-term, lasting prosperity. Shorter terms and short-term limits mean politicians instead choose policies that create seemingly good effects today but lead to bigger crashes and problems tomorrow.

2. Central banks should not be controlled by democratic means. Rather, independent central banks consistently outperform democratically controlled banks. When politicians can push central banks around, they usually chase short-term positions

that lead to long-term disasters, inflation, and recessions.

3. Elected judges, bureaucrats, and administrators consistently perform worse than appointed personnel. Certain technocratic jobs need highly skilled administrators, but citizens are bad at selecting them. Instead, it's better to use, for example, "merit commissions," in which bands of experts deliberate and put forward recommended administrators, who are then chosen by elected officials.

This is just a sampling. Again, note that Jones is not merely stating his own conclusions here, but summarizing the existing literature and showing there is something like a consensus.

Let's take a moment to reflect on one of Jones's examples, an example I have also worked on.[13] The US criminal justice system presents a puzzle: Why is criminal justice in the US so unusually punitive? The US incarcerates people at a much higher rate than almost any other country and gives prisoners unusually long and harsh sentences. People on the Left suspect it's because of racism, but the US criminal justice system of mass incarceration and unusually high levels of generalized violence appeared only when racism waned. Further, overwhelmingly white US states are harsher toward white criminals than most countries are toward minorities. People on the Right usually claim it's because of the breakdown of civil society leading to higher

13. Surprenant and Brennan 2020.

crime. But the US system's punitiveness is not proportional to crime. It indeed started becoming more punitive as crime rose in the 1960s, but it continued to become ever more punitive even once crime started its precipitous fall in the mid-1990s.

It turns out that a significant part of the story has to do with how prosecutors and district attorneys are selected in the US. In the US, but not in most other liberal countries, they are politicians who have to constantly seek reelection. Americans are systematically misinformed about the crime rate (they think there is far more crime than there is, and they think crime is going up even when it's going down), about the effectiveness of jail as a deterrent to crime (they think it's a good deterrent), about the effects of incarceration on criminality (it turns out incarceration reinforces criminal behavior), and so on. Voters reward politicians who pledge to be "tough on crime" even when such measures backfire and make things worse. Anyone who proposes, say, educating or rehabilitating criminals is seen as "soft on crime" and as offering free benefits to criminals which law-abiding citizens do not enjoy. The result is that politicians are in an arms race.[14]

These examples are just examples. I don't necessarily expect you, the reader, to be convinced by any of them. After all, I am merely reporting the conclusions of various research papers, but not carefully walking through the evidence. This isn't a cop-out. Rather, part of the reason is that question of *which issues* should be insulated from political control, period, and which issues should be subject

14. Surprenant and Brennan 2020.

to political control but insulated from democratic control, is too big for one book. A careful look at prison policy takes more than one book. A careful look at central banking takes still more. Examining optimal regulation takes even more.

Thus, my goal in this chapter is not exactly to convince you that we should scale back democracy, or government as a whole, in any of these exact cases. Rather, my goal has been to argue that taking instrumental/epistemic arguments for democracy seriously *requires* the theorist to admit that sometimes it's best not to subject certain issues to political control at all (or only as a reserve power in emergencies), and often, in a generally democratic government, it's best to have many issues insulated from democratic control. Even if you think democracy is overall the best form of government, often less democracy generates better results. Epistemic democrats must grant these points in the abstract, and so it becomes an open debate just how to apply these conclusions. Further, I've argued that *everyone* must be concerned with competent government, because I've given an independent argument for why people have a right not to be subject that all high-stakes decisions be made competently and in good faith.

WHO DECIDES WHO DECIDES?

Political theorists may think they have a ready-made objection to this entire line of argument. They might object that the question of the scope of politics is itself a political question, which therefore must be decided politically. The application of the Epistemic Selection Principle or the Competence Principles are themselves political issues.

Therefore, someone must decide where and how to apply them. There is no "outside the scope of politics" per se, though there may be issues where governments do not regularly and actively control much.

In a published piece replying to her critics, Landemore argues that the question of "who decides" is best decided through democratic means.[15] She says that in specialized cases, democracies will know that it makes sense to turn over certain decisions, such as health regulations or central bank interest rates, to panels of experts rather than deciding directly. She thus acknowledges, as she should, that there are some issues where even a well-functioning deliberative forum of non-experts would be less reliable than a forum of experts.

This may seem to contradict her otherwise strong assertion that the rule of the many always beats decision-making by experts. She saves herself by asserting that the *decision* whether to empower an expert panel is itself best decided by democratic means. So, for her, ultimately democratic bodies are still in charge and hold the fundamental power.[16]

15. Landemore 2016.
16. The economist Arnold Kling remarked that an ideal democracy and an ideal epistocracy would perform equivalently. Assume both a democratic and epistocratic body not only know what they know, but also know their own limits and know when the other body would perform better. In that case, for any decision, they would know whether they should decide for themselves or instead "phone a friend"/ delegate the issue to the wider or narrower body. The interesting question, Kling says, isn't which performs better in principle, but in practice. In practice, which body is

I think this kind of argument is mistaken. Further, epistemic democrats such as Estlund and Landemore cannot accept it, because it is incompatible with their views.

Consider a possible parallel debate between epistemic democrats such as Arneson and Estlund against pure proceduralist democrats, such as Jürgen Habermas or Joshua Cohen. Epistemic democrats, by definition, hold that there are procedure-independent standards for judging the quality or value of political decisions, and part of what justifies particular decision-making methods or institutions is their tendency to track these true standards. The proceduralists claim what counts as right or wrong, good or bad, is something that people debate and disagree about, and conclude that no independent standards bear on the content of those decisions. They try to counter the Epistemic Selection Principle by saying, "Well, *who decides* what the right standards are and whether a particular body or institution meets them? *Someone* has to decide that and *someone* has to create and enforce the various political institutions. Therefore, epistemic theories turn out by necessity to be procedural."

It's true that when writing a constitution, the authors will make a decision about what to include and what to exclude from government control. They will also make a decision about which powers to delegate to whom. When the constitution is ratified, those voting for or against it will in turn make the same kinds of decisions. Nevertheless, this does not imply there is no independent truth of the matter about which topics are properly subject to state

more likely to suffer from the Dunning-Kruger Effect, be overconfident, fall prey to cognitive biases, and so on.

control and which are not, or which powers should be delegated to whom.

Consider, by analogy, if you make a conscious decision to avoid robbing your colleague, you would not conclude that because you decided not to, that there are no external standards by which to judge your behavior, or that the rightness or wrongness of your decision was determined by your choice. Rather, you think your choice not to rob your colleague means you choose to *conform* to pre-existing moral standards. Had you decided to rob your colleague, you would have acted wrongly.

The same point applies to those writing the constitution. When the Soviets decided to instantiate central planning, they decided wrongly, because the government would of course be incompetent to engage in central planning. When the US founders decided to instantiate freedom of religion, they decided rightly, because in fact people have this right and in fact states are not competent to select the correct religion. When someone writes a constitution, they are not deciding by fiat what is properly subject to political control; rather, they are to a large part deciding whether to conform or violate independent principles about what should and should not be subject to political control.

A similar line of argument holds for the question of "who decides who decides"—that is, for the scope of government itself. Thus, when Landemore says that democracy is best fit to decide which issues should be granted under direct democratic or epistocratic rule, she should—for the sake of consistency—be read not as saying that the scope of politics is itself a question only democracy should decide, but rather that—in light of what she takes the empirical and theoretical work on decision-making to show—the

Epistemic Selection Principle tells us that democracies are competent to decide which powers should be delegated to which bodies. She can and indeed must admit that for many issues, there's an independent truth of the matter that they should be left to civil society or the market.

Chapter 4

Alternatives to Democracy

THE PREVIOUS CHAPTER ARGUED THAT one way to deal with democracy's problems was to have less of it. Not everything should be subject to political control; some things are legitimately outside the sphere of politics *because* political decisions are likely to be unreliable. Some things might legitimately be inside the sphere of politics, but only indirectly and tenuously subject to democratic oversight. Instead, these decisions should be delegated or devolved to more reliable and competent decision-makers.

In this chapter, I'll argue that we should be open to experimenting with alternatives to normal electoral democracy which could mitigate the effects of poor political knowledge.

VOTER ACHIEVEMENT DAY: PAY THE PEOPLE TO KNOW

During the 2016 Brexit referendum, polls show that both Remain and Leave voters were systematically misinformed about the relevant facts. Both overestimated what percentage of the UK population consisted of EU immigrants. Both underestimated how much foreign investment in the

Debating Democracy. Jason Brennan and Hélène Landemore, Oxford University Press. © Oxford University Press 2022. DOI: 10.1093/oso/9780197540817.003.0005

UK came from the EU and overestimated how much came from China or elsewhere. Both overestimated how much money the UK sent to the EU for various kinds of redistributive programs. However, while both were systematically wrong, the Leave voters were systematically more in error than the Remain voters.

It's plausible that had voters been better informed, they would have voted to remain rather than leave. In the same way, if you found that a slight majority favors cutting the federal budget but that majority also overestimates the size of the federal budget by a factor of four, you would reasonably suspect their desire to cut the budget is based on their error. Perhaps if they knew the truth, they would not want to cut the budget. They might even want to increase it.

We know that the mean, median, and modal voter is badly informed. We also know that the reason they are badly informed is that they respond rationally to the perverse incentives they face. What if we tried to change the incentives?

One idea would be to increase the power individual voters have. Imagine you selected 100 citizens at random. They, and only they, are allowed to vote. Now, with their votes counting for so much, citizens would have strong incentive to think carefully about their votes, learn the relevant information, and process that information in a careful way.

However, we can reasonably worry any sort of sortition mechanism like this would have serious downsides. The problem seems to be this: When voters' votes don't matter, voters are dumb, but nice. That is, they are ignorant and misinformed, but they at least vote sociotropically, in favor of what they (often mistakenly) believe is the common good. When voters' votes do count, they become smart, but mean. That is, they become better informed, but they vote selfishly.

Political scientists Timothy Feddersen, Sean Gailmard, and Alvaro Sandroni have provided strong empirical evidence in favor of this hypothesis.[1] They conducted economic experiments in which subjects could choose to vote in self-interested or public-spirited ways, with significant sums of real money at stake. They find that when subjects' individual votes had a low probability of being decisive, subjects voted in an unselfish, publicly spirited way. In games where subjects' individual votes had high probabilities of being decisive, subjects voted for narrow self-interest at the expense of the common good.

Concentrating votes among the few is dangerous. Spreading them among the many is dangerous. What if instead try to nudge the many to be just a bit better informed? Bryan Caplan recently proposed an alternative mechanism to do just that.

Call it National Voter Achievement Day. Here's how it works. A few weeks before an election or referendum takes place, voters may voluntarily go to a testing center. They will be given, say, a fifty-question quiz of basic political information, asking them questions such as who their representatives are, which party controls various houses, what some recent major bills were, how much money is spent on this or that, questions about recent events, and questions about social indicators (such as the unemployment rate).

---

1. Feddersen, Gailmard, and Sandroni 2009.

Perhaps 200–300 such questions are posted online ahead of time, but during the test, citizens get fifty at random.

Citizens who get, say, 90–100% of the questions right get a $1000 tax credit. Citizens who get 80–89% get $500. Citizens who get 70–79 get $100. Anything lower, and you get nothing. Here, the idea isn't that passing the test determines who votes. Rather, it's that you acquire a financial incentive to know this basic information.

Neither Caplan nor I expect Voter Achievement Day to solve all of our problems. But it should at least nudge voters in the right direction. They are ignorant because they are incentivized to be ignorant. We might be able to induce them to at least know the basics. Again, it seems implausible that Brexit would have occurred if British citizens knew the basic facts.

ENLIGHTENED PREFERENCE VOTING

Recall a problem I mentioned briefly in the opening chapter. Suppose we poll a number of citizens. We find that the more knowledgeable citizens tend to support free trade, while the less knowledgeable support protectionism. It's tempting to conclude immediately that their different attitudes are explained by the different levels of knowledge. However, we have to be careful. After all, the two groups may be distinct in other ways. Perhaps these other factors, rather than knowledge, explain the different attitudes.

Note that this worry goes the other way, too. If you show me that white voters tend to prefer X, but black voters tend to prefer Y, that is not enough to show that *race* explains the difference. It could be that race has no independent effect at all, but confounding factors—such as differences in education, income, geography, or knowledge—create the appearance of a racial distinction.

The only way to know is to measure, check, and correct for these confounds. Fortunately, as I mentioned in chapter 1, this point is nothing new. In fact, political scientists and economists working on the issue of voter attitudes regularly measure and correct for such factors. You need to collect three sets of data:

1. What people know
2. What they want
3. Who they are

With these three sets of data, you can determine how what people know affects what they want while controlling for who they are. This allows us to confidently conclude, for instance, that more knowledgeable people favor free trade, while more ignorant people favor protectionism, and what explains the difference is indeed *knowledge* rather than income or some other factor.

With such data, you can also statistically estimate what a *fully informed* demographically identical public would want. Bryan Caplan summarizes the method as follows:

1. Administer a survey of policy preferences *combined with* a test of objective political knowledge.
2. Statistically estimate individuals' policy preferences as a function of their objective political knowledge and their demographics—such as income, race, and gender.

3. Simulate what policy preferences *would* look like if all members of all demographic groups had the *maximum* level of objective political knowledge.[2]

Doing so allows you to estimate the public's *enlightened preferences*: what the electorate would have wanted if it had gotten a perfect score on the knowledge test.

Note that you can do other simulations. You can estimate what a demographically identical public would want if it were completely uninformed or misinformed in particular ways. You can estimate what the public would want if it were all male or all female, all white or all back, all rich or all poor, or if it had no demographics at all.

Note also that this method does not a priori guarantee convergence. If our simulated enlightened public prefers X rather than Y, this is an interesting result. After all, it could be that a simulated enlightened public is agnostic, or has radical divergence, or something else.

This kind of method is imperfect. We can reasonably worry that we would have gotten different results with different questions. We can reasonably worry that chopping up demographic categories differently would produce different results. Nevertheless, it's worth noting that many different researchers, using the same kind of method but with different tests of knowledge and different sets of data, tend to converge on the same sorts of results, such as that an enlightened public favors free trade over protectionism, is more tolerant and open, is more open to immigration, and favors diplomacy over militaristic interventions.[3]

---

2. Caplan 2007, 25.
3. Caplan 2007; Althaus 2003.

Further, if we're worried that a different battery of questions would produce different results, we can, well, check by running a new study.

Enlightened preference voting is a possible voting system that utilizes this research method in attempt to produce higher quality government. On Election Day, everyone gets to participate, and participate as an equal. However, when they participate, they do not merely vote for a candidate, party, or position on a referendum. Rather, they have to do three things:

1. Tell us who they are, by indicating their demographic information, such as sex, gender identity, income level, ethnicity, employment status, and so on. If we are worried about people lying about these things (we apparently are not when we take the census), we might give everyone a government-issued voter ID card which contains this information.

2. Tell us what they know. Citizens will take, say, a thirty-question quiz of basic political information (more on that below). No cell phones allowed; it's not an open-book exam.

3. Tell us what they want, for example, which candidate or party they support in an election, or which position they support in a referendum.

Note that this test of knowledge is *not* used to determine who gets to vote and who doesn't. Rather, the idea is that once we have all three sets of data, the data is anonymized and released to the public domain. The government electoral commission then uses the data to estimate, via predetermined methods, what the public *would have wanted* if it were demographically identical but had gotten a perfect score on the knowledge test. This result—the public's enlightened preference—is then instantiated. For instance, if the enlightened public favors Remain but the actual public favors Leave, the country remains. Since the data is public, the government's calculations can easily be verified or challenged.

A democrat might reasonably say that enlightened preference voting, rather than being an alternative to democracy, is really a better *form* of democracy. When we participate, we participate equally. It's not exactly the case that more knowledgeable participants get extra votes. There is a sense in which we could, in principle, *after* the enlightened preference calculation is done, make a rough estimate about whether Bob had in effect 3.7 votes while Tom had 1.2. But even this is artificial. It's a bit like trying to estimate how much of an effect some particular year of schooling has on life expectancy while controlling for genes, diet, and exercise, except, in this case, we can't really say which year of schooling corresponds to Bob in the analogy. A better way to put it is that we all have equal influence on the voting system, which then generates a prediction about what we would have wanted if we were better informed. For that reason, a democrat might decide to champion enlightened preference voting. Rather than saying it's a way of crushing the masses, it's a better mechanism for extracting wisdom from the crowd.

On the other hand, we might instead conclude that enlightened preference voting is not really a form of democracy. It depends on how much substance we need to build into the word "democracy." On some popular theoretical definitions, a system is democratic only if the people collectively rule themselves. In a way, in enlightened preference voting, they do not really rule themselves. Rather, a kind of constructed or simulated public rules the actual public. For this reason, we might want to say that enlightened preference voting is not really a form of democracy at all. (By this logic, it is also not technically a form of epistocracy—that is, a system in which the informed have more power than others. After all, in enlightened preference voting, a constructed public rules, not the actual well-informed people.)

Enlightened preference voting does not attempt to build better voters. It doesn't require that we educate them more. While it cannot overcome all forms of bias, it at least helps us examine and eliminate demographic biases in voting behavior (more on that below). It doesn't require that we somehow turn Hobbits and Hooligans into Vulcans. The goal is to build something straight from the crooked timber of humanity without having to straighten voters out.

WHO DECIDES WHAT COUNTS AS ENLIGHTENED?

Though David Estlund is a democrat, he accepts that "removing the right issues from democratic control and turning them over to the right experts would lead to better political decisions, and more justice and prosperity."[4] He accepts some citizens have more moral–political expertise than others, and that some people are better judges of

---

4. Estlund 2007, 262.

morality and justice than others, too.[5] Indeed, he thinks it would be unreasonable to claim that all citizens are equally competent.

But, Estlund says, there is a problem. Any particular conception of competence is bound to be controversial. Estlund continues: "The trick is knowing . . . which experts to rely on for which issues."[6] He says, "Any *particular* person or group who might be put forward as such an expert would be subject to . . . controversy."[7]

Now, Estlund does not mean to say that if something is controversial, then there is no truth of the matter and nothing can be done about it. After all, his own philosophical defense of democracy—and the premises it relies upon—is controversial, with lots of (indeed, most) reasonable people disputing it.

Rather, he thinks that any sort of test of competence— or the choice of any panel of experts—must itself be

5. Note also that democrats tend to favor universal public education in part because they think such education is needed to make citizens prepared to participate in politics. They also typically favor having citizens make decisions after reasoned public discourse and deliberation, rather than on spur-of-the-moment emotions. Most democrats are thus already committed to the view that some citizens have better moral and political knowledge than others. After all, some of us have received and internalized good political education, while others have not. Some of us have engaged in reasoned public discourse and deliberation, while others have not. Given their commitments to deliberation and education, democratic theorists would be hard-pressed to argue that *all* adult citizens are already politically competent.
6. Estlund 2007, 262.
7. Estlund 2007, 36.

publicly justifiable. He thinks that all reasonable people can and should accept in the *abstract* that there are real distinctions among political experts, the merely competent, and the incompetent. Estlund also thinks that citizens can agree to *abstract* claims about competence—for example, that competent decision-makers use relevant evidence while incompetent decision-makers tend to ignore it. However, he thinks that any particular, specific, *concrete* way of making these distinctions will be subject to reasonable objections.[8] There is no particular way of making these distinctions which all reasonable people must accept on pain of irrationality. He thinks this creates a major barrier to justifying any form of epistocracy.

Another related worry goes as follows: In the real world, if we try to instantiate enlightened preference voting, we will have to empower real-world actors to write the 30-question knowledge exam. It's one thing when some political scientist uses the enlightened preference method to study political psychology, when nothing is at stake other than some scientific hypothesis. But if these exams were used to determine political outcomes, then politicians, partisans, bureaucrats, and special interest groups would try to game the exam to favor their preferred outcomes. In the real world, we're going to have to put the task of deciding who counts as competent in someone's hands. That person might be incompetent to decide who counts as competent or might use this power in bad faith.

I think the same institutional response can overcome both worries. What goes on the test? Answer: Have the

8. Estlund 2007, 71, passim.

citizens decide using a deliberative poll. A month or so before preference voting day takes place, randomly select, say, five hundred citizens from around the country. Pay them to spend a few days deliberating to design the thirty-question battery of questions. Require their employers not to penalize them. We can use a democratic decision method to choose the set of questions which go on the knowledge portion of the exam.

You might think this seems like a paradoxical thing for me to say. Haven't I been arguing that deliberation often fails or makes things worse, and that crowds don't have wisdom? But we need to be careful here. I haven't argued crowds are always and everywhere subject to systematic errors, or that political partisanship makes us stupid and blind about everything. Rather, crowds make systematic errors about some issues—such as immigration, trade economics, or war—but are wise about others—such as the number of jellybeans in a jar.

The average citizen can and does have a *reasonable* concrete theory of competence. Most citizens have good and reasonable intuitions about political competence. They have pretty good ideas about what it takes to be informed, about what kinds of information a voter needs to know, and so on. As a group, they can deliver a reasonable account of political competence.

The empirical literature on voter irrationality and ignorance does not say that voters have bad standards, but rather that they are bad at *applying* their reasonable standards.[9] There is nothing particularly unusual about this.

---

9. Caplan 2007 claims that voters tend to vote for candidates whom they believe will promote the national common good

My children are not yet competent to choose a marriage partner, but if you ask them to describe in the abstract what makes for a good spouse, they can give you a good account. Students who receive low scores on final exams frequently know what kinds of information they ought to have to pass, even though they lack that information. For instance, I might know that I need to memorize twenty trigonometric identities but fail the exam because, well, I didn't actually memorize them. So it goes with citizens. They know that a well-informed citizen should know who their representative is and who controls congress, even though most of them don't know these things. Citizens have a pretty good grasp of the questions, if not the answers.

The question, "What should an informed electorate know?" is easy to answer. *Being informed* is hard. Questions about identifying standards of competence are easy even if becoming competent is hard. Most citizens can identify what it takes for a medical doctor to be competent even if they themselves might be unable to pass medical school exams.

Voters know senators should not be blamed for weather, even though, when they actually vote, citizens tend to punish incumbents for bad weather.[10] Voters know that politicians are not to blame for international events beyond their control. Yet, when voters actually vote, they

---

and increase national prosperity. However, voters are irrational in how they evaluate candidates by this standard. Voters have the right standards for selecting candidates, but are terrible at applying these standards. See also the previous endnote.

10. Healy and Mahotra 2010.

actually do punish incumbents for international events beyond their control.[11] Voters know that good-looking candidates aren't better candidates, but nevertheless they tend to vote for the better-looking candidates.[12] Voters are more trustworthy and reliable in being asked to articulate what makes someone a good candidate than being asked to identify actual good candidates. They are better at coming up with standards than applying them. So, there is good reason to hold democracy is incompetent to decide certain economic and political policies and yet could be competent to decide what counts as competence.

Some ardent democrats agree with this very point. For instance, Thomas Christiano used to favor a political system in which citizens would choose the ends of government, but were not tasked with voting for the *means*.[13] His argument was that they are competent to do the former but not the latter, since the latter requires highly specialized social scientific knowledge.

Now consider David Estlund's challenge. He says that while in the abstract, we can and should all accept the idea of there being a real distinction between informed, ignorant, and misinformed voters, there is no *particular, concrete* way of articulating this distinction which all reasonable people must accept. He might be right, but this doesn't stop the conversation.

On the contrary, this situation is ubiquitous. Take any abstract principles of justice or any abstract view

---

11. Leigh 2009.
12. Todorov, Mandisodza, Goren, and Hall 2005; Ballew and Todorov 2007, 17948–17953; Lenz and Lawson 2008.
13. Christiano 2008, 104. Emphasis mine.

about which goals democracy ought to promote. Even if, say, all reasonably can and must agree that, say, freedom of religious expression takes priority over freedom of commercial expression, any *particular, concrete, and specific* way of interpreting or instantiating this principle will be controversial, with some reasonable people disputing it. Similarly, Gerald Gaus argues that liberals can conclusively justify a social minimum, but they cannot conclusively justify any particular, concrete theory of the social minimum.[14] Reasonable people will reasonably dispute whether a given legal, concrete account of the social minimum is too low or too high. Even if all reasonable people think a just basic structure must ensure, one way or another, that everyone has enough, what counts as "enough," and even what counts as "ensuring" is controversial and indeterminate from the standpoint of public reason.

The same goes for pretty much every political idea. The problem Estlund poses—that a principle might be acceptable to all reasonable people in the abstract, but any concrete interpretation will be controversial—is *normal*. It applies not merely to the question of what counts as political competence, but most everything else.

So, Estlund has a dilemma here. He could say that unless we can show that a particular, concrete interpretation of some abstract idea *must* be accepted by every reasonable person, then we are forbidden to instantiate any concrete law or policy. But, since this problem is ubiquitous for every political principle, this would force Estlund

14. Gaus 2004, 193.

to be some sort of anarchist rather than a proponent of the democratic state. Alternatively, what Estlund can—and I think must—say, is that if some principle is justifiable in the abstract, but any particular interpretation is controversial, we should rely on a fair and reliable umpire to adjudicate it.

Let's put this more precisely. When we can agree on abstract principles but disagree on the correct concrete interpretation of those principles, then this gives us grounds for seeking a good way to adjudicate our disputes. We should submit our dispute (about the best interpretation of that principle) to a good umpire.[15] On this very point, Gaus argues—and it seems plausible to me—that a good umpire is:

1. Impartial/Fair: Umpires must not be biased toward or against any particular side.
2. Reliable/Competent: Umpires must have a sufficiently high ability to make correct decisions and arrive at the truth.
3. Decisive: Umpires should reach decisions quickly.
4. Public: Those bound by the umpire's decisions should be able to recognize that the umpire has features 1–3.[16]

15. It is worth noting here that this is why Gaus prefers democracy. He believes some principles can be publicly justified, and democracy is a fair and reliable method for adjudicating among our competing interpretations of publicly justified principles.
16. This summarizes Gaus 1996, 184–191.

Note that an "umpire" here could refer to a person, group of people, or any other decision-making method (such as flipping a coin).

Estlund's own work is meant to show that democratic decision-making is a largely fair, decisive, and public decision-making process, which all people can accept. Whether it is competent for a given decision depends upon the issue. Thus, I think Estlund can accept my proposal in this chapter—indeed, he may even insist that it qualifies as a kind of democracy.

To review, Estlund agrees that in the abstract, we all can and should recognize that some people know more than others, and that there is a real distinction between political competence and incompetence. However, he claims, we cannot prove conclusively, to all reasonable people, that any particular, concrete way of making this distinction is the correct one. Rather than throwing up our hands, I have argued, he can—indeed, it appears must—instead say that all this shows is that we should submit the question of how to operationalize the distinction between incompetence and competence to a fair, reliable, decisive, and public umpire. In this case, a democratic deliberative poll is just such an umpire.

IT DOESN'T HAVE TO BE PERFECT. IT JUST HAS TO BE BETTER.

Enlightened preference voting is not perfect. We won't know how to test every form of information needed to vote well. A thirty-question battery of basic information is highly imperfect. It won't screen for political bias and irrationality. It might not directly test advanced social scientific knowledge, knowledge which is crucial to voting well but which is not easily verifiable.

Nevertheless, the system does not have to be perfect. It just needs to be *better*.

In the past, Landemore has expressed some skepticism about whether enlightened preference methods really do tend to track the truth, or track the truth *better* than unenlightened voting. She complains that just because a simulated well-informed electorate has different policy preferences than a badly informed electorate, this does not entail, logically that the well informed are right.[17] She's right—it's possible the "enlightened public" is wrong and the actual, unenlightened public is correct.

However, we have to ask what's most probable, rather than what's merely possible. The argument for why we should place greater trust in enlightened preference voting goes as follows.

Some of the basic political information tested by survey devices such as the National Election Studies is directly useful for forming sound political judgments. Some is not. If a deliberative poll were to construct a thirty-question battery, they would likely ask similar questions, such as which parties control what, what parties plan to do, what various social indicators are, what the budget contains, what laws have been passed, and perhaps what the price of a local bus ticket is, among other things. Strictly speaking, a person could know all of this stuff but have poor political judgment, while it's logically possible a person could lack

17. Landemore 2012, 200.

this information and yet somehow still know which candidates, policies, or platforms are best.

However, over and over again we find that high scores on basic, objective political knowledge are correlated with systematically different political beliefs than low scores. This is a surprising empirical result—the results could have come out differently. Highly informed people have systematically different opinions than badly informed people. Even highly informed people inside different parties tend to agree with each other more than they agree with badly informed people inside their own parties. Again, *none of this* is explained by demographic factors or demographic biases, such as income or race, because we have tested and controlled for that. Thus, the best explanation for these differences is that knowing basic political information is positively *correlated* with having the kind of social scientific and philosophical knowledge that is relevant and necessary to form sound and justified political beliefs.

Thus, a country's *enlightened preferences* are much more likely to be sound than the country's *actual, unenlightened preferences*. There is no guarantee, but no one is asking for a guarantee. Nevertheless, in the absence of actual evidence to the contrary, we should let the enlightened preferences be our guide.

Consider: We survey, say, 130 million Americans on election day. We ask them who the president is, who is the vice president, what the unemployment rate is, which party controls congress, who their representative is, and so on. We then can run some calculations and say, "If a demographically identical population had scored a perfect thirty out of thirty on this quiz, they would support the free-trade candidate over the protectionist by a 40% margin."

That isn't *proof* that the free-trade candidate is a better one, but it's compelling evidence nonetheless.

Further, the quality of candidates, what platforms parties run, and even which parties exist are not independent variables. The quality of our choices depends upon the quality of the voters. If voters are largely ignorant, biased, and misinformed, this to some degree condemns parties to having to cater to their biases; though, as we discussed in chapter 1, if voters are ignorant enough, unopinionated enough, and have bad memories, it also to some degree liberates parties to ignore most voters and do as they please. However, to win in an enlightened preference system, candidates have to cater to a simulated enlightened electorate. Since the knowledge quiz is determined only shortly before the election, and since the quiz is not released to the public until they walk into the polls, they will have to up their game ahead of time, without being able to game their policies to the quiz.

Now, if we were to implement this policy in the real world, I would expect various politicians, special interest groups, and others to try to game the system as much as they can. I suggested we set the questions via deliberative polling, but my worries about deliberative polling from chapter 2 still remain.

Indeed, this is one reason why I want to combine such polling with enlightened preference voting, rather than merely rely on deliberative polls. Voting puts a check on the 500 test-designers' power, and thus reduces the damage motivated or biased moderators might do. Further, the poll is asked to do a simple task (pick questions to test political knowledge), rather than a hard task, such as choose trade policy.

Indeed, real-life democracies are subject to all sorts of abuse. Politicians rig voting systems and voting districts to favor their parties. Laws limiting advertising and spending are often for the benefit of incumbents. Rent-seeking is common.

For me, the issue isn't whether an enlightened preference system will be free of such problems. Of course, it won't be. Rather, the issue is whether, all things considered, it will perform *better* than our current system of unenlightened voting. Which system, warts and all, will produce the most just outcomes, do the best job respecting and protecting people's liberal freedoms, be the most stable, and most contribute to growth and prosperity?

I wouldn't recommend we change all at once. The best bet is to experiment on a small scale. Perhaps one small country or one small state might experiment with enlightened preference voting. If it works, we can scale it up. If it doesn't, we modify it to work out the kinks. If we can't do that, we try something else.

DEMOCRACY'S RACE PROBLEM: WHY ENLIGHTENED PREFERENCE VOTING IS BETTER FOR MINORITIES

One major advantage of enlightened preference voting over standards forms of democracy is that it can overcome and control for the problem of demographic bias in democratic elections. Democracy empowers everyone equally, but when it comes to voting, people tend to think and act as members of political *teams*. What happens when they see their *race* as their team?

In modern democracies, including democracies with compulsory voting, the voting electorate is not demographically identical to the eligible electorate or to the citizenry as a whole. Advantaged voters, such as men, high-income citizens, the middle-aged, and so on vote at higher rates than disadvantaged voters.[18] Even though the evidence overwhelmingly shows that citizens vote sociotropically rather than for their narrow self-interest, one might still reasonably worry that political outcomes will not properly reflect the interests of all. Many democrats worry about this problem even though they are far more sanguine about political irrationality, ignorance, and misinformation than I am.[19]

On this point, Thomas Christiano raises the problem of what he calls "persistent minorities":

> This problem is the difficulty of persistent minorities. There is a persistent minority in a democratic society when that minority always loses in the voting. This is always a possibility in democracies because of the use of majority rule. If the society is divided into two or more highly unified voting blocks in which the members of each group votes in the same ways as all the other members of that group, then the group in the minority will find itself always on the losing end of the votes. This problem has plagued some societies, particularly those with indigenous peoples who live within developed societies. Though this problem is often connected with majority tyranny it is distinct from the problem of majority tyranny because it may be the case that the majority

18. Delli-Carpini and Keeter 1996; Hill 2002; Somin 2013; Brennan and Hill 2014.
19. E.g., Estlund 2007.

attempts to treat the minority well, in accordance with its
conception of good treatment. It is just that the minority
never agrees with the majority on what constitutes proper
treatment. Being a persistent minority can be highly oppressive even if the majority does not try to act oppressively.
This can be understood with the help of the very ideas that
underpin democracy. Persons have interests in being able to
correct for the cognitive biases of others and to be able to
make the world in such a way that it makes sense to them.
These interests are set back for a persistent minority since
they never get their way.[20]

Persistent minorities here could include ideological minorities, ethnic minorities, religious minorities, or any other
group who will see their goals continually thwarted simply
because they are small.

To illustrate the problem with an extreme case, imagine again a deeply racist society in which 90% of people are
white and 10% black. Suppose that blacks are not allowed
to vote. Suppose that while the white majority has various
disputes and disagreements, they nevertheless agree that
blacks' interests matter little, and are happy to pass legislation that thwarts their interests. Suppose, however, that
a civil rights movement succeeds in getting equal voting
rights for black citizens. Now, blacks can vote, and every
black citizen is equal to every white. However, because
whites form a supermajority, they nevertheless persistently thwart blacks' interests. In turns out blacks only
have influence when whites are divided.

Robert Nozick used an example like this in a parable
called the "Tale of the Slave." He asked readers to imagine

20. https://plato.stanford.edu/entries/democracy/.

a situation in which, over time, a person who started as a slave was eventually granted full voting rights. However, what was disturbing about Nozick's example was that, in the end, that person still only had influence, efficacy, or power when the other voters were split 5000 to 5000. Since that never happened, the upshot was that granting the slave full voting rights didn't really improve his situation. To say that granting him the right to vote set him free is something of a joke.[21] Being a member of a rule-making body, especially a large one, does not give one much control. You are at others' mercy.

I don't mean to suggest things are this bad in most democracies. Nevertheless, the point is that enfranchising a minority group as equals is not sufficient to guarantee it gets a say or gets treated as an equal. Minorities remain at the mercy of majorities.

Enlightened preference voting already allows us to simulate what a demographically identical public *would* have supported had it been fully informed. It offers still further value. Using the same statistical methods, we can actually check for, measure, and even *correct* various kinds of racial, ethnic, or demographic bias. We can model different kinds of fully informed electorates. We can determine how the public would have voted if it were fully informed and all black, or all white.

We can go even further. John Rawls famously had the idea that, to determine what justice requires, we should imagine bargainers choosing rules of social interaction that will bind them. However, to make the bargain fair, he

21. Nozick 1974.

asks us to imagine that the bargainers know only general facts about people. They do not know their own race, gender, age, conception of the good life, income level, class, religion, hobbies, or other personal attributes. Thus, when they choose the rules, they end up choosing for everyone. They cannot bias the rules toward their own narrow interests—because they don't know who they in particular are—and so end up choosing rules which are good for everybody, regardless of what their particular personal characteristics are like.[22]

Enlightened preference voting could allow us to mimic Rawls's veil of ignorance for whatever decision we throw at it. Instead of estimating what a demographical identical but fully informed public would have wanted, we would estimate what a fully informed public would have wanted if *all demographic effects were neutralized*. In principle, we could do a great deal to purge democratic decision-making of class, race, income, or geographic bias.

Now, it's an open question whether doing so would be good or not. Some philosophers and theorists dispute whether a veil of ignorance, rather than defeating unfair biases, instead removes important information. I am not taking a firm stand here. Rather, my more important point is that democracy, as it stands, is full of such biases. Further, it empowers majorities or pluralities at the expense of minorities and the few. These minorities remain at the mercy of the majorities, because equal voting rights means their block gets its way only when the majority, in effect, lets it, either by being split, indifferent,

22. Rawls 1971.

or simply open. While democracies—thanks to their tight connection to liberalism—tend in fact to be more open, tolerant, and respectful of minority rights, they do not go far enough. Enlightened preference voting can go further to fix the problem.

OTHER ALTERNATIVES AND CONCLUSION

Democracy tends to perform better than the alternative systems we have tried. But the other systems we've tried have been awful, so it is a low bar. Democracy nevertheless has systematic flaws. It empowers We the People to rule but simultaneously incentivizes us to rule foolishly, to indulge our worst biases, and to succumb to ignorance and misinformation.

This does not merely mean that democracy underperforms. Rather, the political power the electorate wields matters. When we vote badly—as we usually do—economic opportunities vanish or fail to materialize. We fight unjust wars. We waste trillions of dollars on programs that don't work and fail to spend money on programs that do. We inflict and perpetuate injustice. We leave the poor behind. We trample civil and economic liberties.

Exercising such power incompetently is not merely harmful; it's evil. It remains evil even when we do it together, as equals.

I am skeptical that the problems of democracy can be fixed with more democracy. Democratic deliberation does not usually seem to work as its proponents contend. The idea that we can make democracies smarter just by adding more voters seems false.

Nevertheless, the goal should be to fix what's wrong with democracy as much as possible. Over the past two chapters, I've offered a few major ideas. One is to reduce the scope of politics. A second is to keep democracy but outsource more decisions to experts and others. A third is to pay citizens to know more. A fourth is to use enlightened preference voting to estimate what We the People would have wanted if only We the People knew what we were talking about. There are other ideas out there as well worth trying that I haven't touched upon. Still, regardless of democracy's past successes, we have an obligation—founded on justice—to acknowledge and overcome its systematic failings.

REFERENCES

Acemoglu, Daron, and James Robinson. 2013. *Why Nations Fail.* London: Profile.

Achen, Christopher, and Larry Bartels. 2002. "Blind Retrospection: Electoral Responses to Draught, Flue, and Shark Attacks." Prepared for presentation at the annual meeting of the American Political Science Association, Boston.

Achen, Christopher, and Larry Bartels. 2016. *Democracy for Realists.* Princeton: Princeton University Press.

Ackerman, Bruce, and James Fishkin. 2005. *Deliberation Day.* New Haven: Yale University Press.

Alesina, A., Spolaore, E., and R. Wacziarg. 2005. "Trade, Growth, and the Size of Countries," *Handbook of Economic Growth* 1: 1499–1542.

Althaus, Scott. 1998. "Information Effects in Collective Preferences," *American Political Science Review* 92: 545–558.

Althaus, Scott. 2003. *Collective Preferences in Democratic Politics.* New York: Cambridge University Press.

Alvarez, Michael. 1997. *Information and Elections.* Ann Arbor: University of Michigan Press.

Arian, Asher, and Schamir, Michal. 1983. "The Primarily Political Functions of the Left-Right Continuum," *Comparative Politics* 15: 139–158.

Arceneaux, Kevin, and Robert M. Stein. 2006. "Who Is held Responsible When Disaster Strikes? The Attribution of Responsibility for a Natural Disaster in an Urban Election," *Journal of Urban Affairs* 28: 43–53.

Ballew, II, Charles C., and Alexander Todorov. 2007. "Predicting Political Elections from Rapid and Unreflective Face Judgments," *Proceedings of the National Academy of Sciences* 104: 17948–17953.

Barber, Michael, and Jeremy Pope. 2018. "Does Party Trump Ideology: Disentangling Party and Ideology in America" *American Political Science Review* 113: 1–17.

Barnes, Samuel H. 1971. "Left, Right, and the Italian Voter," *Comparative Political Studies* 4: 157–175.

Bartels, Larry. 1986. "Issue Voting under Uncertainty: An Empirical Test," *American Journal of Political Science* 30: 709–728.

Bartels, Larry. 1996. "Uninformed Votes: Information Effects in Presidential Elections," *American Political Science Review* 40: 194–230.

Bartels, Larry. 2003. "Democracy with Attitudes." In George Rabinowitz and Michael B. MacKeun, eds., *Electoral Democracy*. New York: Oxford University Press, 48–81.

Bostrom, Nick, and Toby Ord. 2006. "The Reversal Test: Eliminating Status Quo Bias in Applied Ethics," *Ethics* 116: 656–679.

Brennan, Geoffrey, and Loren Lomasky. 1993. *Democracy and Decision*. New York: Cambridge University Press.

Brennan, Jason. 2011. "Condorcet's Jury Theorem and the Optimum Number of Voters," *Politics* 31: 55–62.

Brennan, Jason. 2013. "Epistocracy within Public Reason," in Ann Cudd and Sally Scholz, eds., *Democracy in the Twenty-First Century*. Berlin: Springer, 191–204.

Brennan, Jason. 2016a. *Against Democracy*. Princeton University Press.

Brennan, Jason. 2016b. "Democracy and Freedom." In David Schmidtz and Carmen Pavel, eds., *Oxford Handbook of Freedom*. Oxford University Press, 335–349.

Brennan, Jason, and Lisa Hill. 2014. *Compulsory Voting: For and Against*. New York: Cambridge University Press.

Cagé, Julia. 2020. "Media Competition, Information Provision and Political Participation: Evidence from French Local Newspapers and Elections, 1944–2014," *Journal of Public Economics* 185: 104–177.

Campbell, Angus, Converse, Philip E., Miller, Warren E., and Donald E. Stokes. 1960. *The American Voter*. New York: John Wiley.

Caplan, Bryan. 2007. *The Myth of the Rational Voter: Why Democracies Choose Bad Policies*. Princeton: Princeton University Press.

Caplan, Bryan, Crampton, Eric, Grove, Wayne A., and Ilya Somin. 2013. "Systematically Biased Beliefs about Political Influence: Evidence from the Perceptions of Political Influence on Policy Outcomes Survey," *PS: Political Science and Politics* 46: 760–767.

Carter, John, and Stephen Guerette. 1992. "An Experimental Study of Expressive Voting," *Public Choice* 73: 251–260.

Chong, Dennis. 2013. "Degrees of Rationality in Politics." In David O. Sears and Jack S. Levy, eds., *The Oxford Handbook of Political Psychology*. New York: Oxford University Press, 96–129.

Christiano, Thomas. 2008. *The Constitution of Equality*. New York: Oxford University Press.

Christiano, Thomas. 2015. "Voter Ignorance Is Not Necessarily a Problem," *Critical Review* 27: 253–269.

Cohen, E. G. 1982. "Expectation States and Interracial Interaction in School Settings," *Annual Review of Sociology* 8: 209–235.

Cohen, Geoffrey. 2003. "Party over Policy: The Dominating Impact of Group Influence on Political Beliefs," *Journal of Personality and Social Psychology* 85: 808–822.

Colombo, C., and M. R. Steenbergen. 2020. "Heuristics and Biases in Political Decision Making." In William Thompson, ed., *Oxford Research Encyclopedia of Politics*, https://www.oxfordhandbooks.com/view/10.1093/oxfordhb/9780190634131.001.0001/oxfordhb-9780190634131-e-9. New York: Oxford University Press.

Converse, Philip. 1964. "The Nature of Belief Systems in Mass Publics." In D. E. Apter, ed., *Ideology and Discontent*. London: Free Press of Glencoe, 206–61.

Converse, Philip. 1990. "Popular Representation and the Distribution of Information." In John A. Ferejohn and James H. Kuklinski, eds., *Information and Democratic Processes*. Urbana: University of Illinois Press, 369–88.

Converse, Philip, and Pierce, Richard. 1986. *Political Representation in France*. Cambridge MA: Harvard University Press.

Curato, N., Dryzek, J. S., Ercan, S. A., Hendriks, C. M., and S. Niemeyer. 2017. "Twelve Key Findings in Deliberative Democracy Research," *Daedalus* 146: 28–38.

Danzinger, Shai, Levav, Jonathan, and Liora Avniam-Pesso. 2011. "Extraneous Factors in Judicial Decisions," *PNAS* 108: 6889–6892.

Delli Carpini, Michael X., and Scott Keeter. 1991. "Stability and Change in the US Public's Knowledge of Politics," *Public Opinion Quarterly* 55(1991): 583–612.

Delli Carpini, Michael X., and Scott Keeter. 1996. *What Americans Know about Politics and Why It Matters*. New Haven: Yale University Press.

Downs, Donald. 1989. *The New Politics of Pornography*. Chicago: University of Chicago Press.

Dryzek, J. S., Bächtiger, A., Chambers, S., Cohen, J., Druckman, J. N., Felicetti, A., Fishkin, J.S., Farrell, D.M., Fung, A., Gutmann, A. and Landemore, H., 2019. "The Crisis of Democracy and the Science of Deliberation," *Science*, 363, 1144–1146.

Dynes, Adam, and John Holbein. 2019. "Noisy Introspection: The Effect of Party Control on Policy Outcomes," *American Political Science Review* 114: 237–257.

Ellsworth, Phoebe C. 1989. "Are Twelve Heads Better Than One." *Law and Contemporary Problems* 52: 205–24.

Erison, Cengiz, Lodge, Milton, and Charles S. Taber. 2014. "Affective Contagion in Effortful Political Thinking," *Political Psychology* 35(2014): 187–206.

Estlund, David. 2008. *Democratic Authority*. Princeton: Princeton University Press.

Feddersen, Timothy, Gailmard, Sean, and Alvaro Sandroni. 2009. "A Bias toward Unselfishness in Large Elections: Theory and Experimental Evidence," *American Political Science Review* 103: 175–92.

Ferejohn, John A. 1990. "Introduction." In John Ferejohn and James Kuklinski, eds., *Information and Democratic Processes*. Urbana: University of Illinois Press, 1–7.

Friedman, Jeffrey. 2006. "Democratic Competence in Normative and Positive Theory: Neglected Implications of 'The Nature of Belief Systems in Mass Publics,'" *Critical Review* 18: i–xliii.

Gamm, Gerald H. 1989. *The Making of New Deal Democrats: Voting Behavior and Realignment in Boston, 1920–1940*. Chicago: University of Chicago Press.

Gaus, Gerald. 1996. *Justificatory Liberalism*. New York: Oxford University Press.

Gaus, Gerald. 2004. *Contemporary Theories of Liberalism*. Thousand Oaks: Sage.

Gilens, Martin. 2012. *Affluence and Influence*. Princeton: Princeton University Press.

Goren, Paul. 2005. "Party Identification and Core Political Values," *American Journal of Political Science* 49: 882–897.

Green, Donald, and Ian Shapiro. 1994. *Pathologies of Rational Choice Theory*. New Haven: Yale University Press.

Greene, Steven. 1999. "Understanding Party Identification: A Social Identity Approach," *Political Psychology* 20: 393–403.

Grossback, L. J., Peterson, D. A. M., and J. A. Stimson. 2006. *Mandate Politics*, Cambridge University Press.

Grossback, L. J., Peterson, D. A. M., and J. A. Stimson. 2007. "Electoral Mandates in American Politics," *British Journal of Political Science* 37: 711–730.

Guerrero, Alexander. 2014. "Against Elections: The Lottocratic Alternative," *Philosophy and Public Affairs* 42: 135–178.

Habermas, Jürgen. 2001. *Moral Consciousness and Communicative Action*. Cambridge, MA: MIT Press.

Haidt, Jonathan. 2012. *The Righteous Mind*. New York: Pantheon.

Hardin, Russell. 2009. *How Do You Know?: The Economics of Ordinary Knowledge*. Princeton: Princeton University Press.

Healy, Andrew, and Neil Malholtra. 2010. "Random Events, Economic Losses, and Retrospective Voting: Implications for Democratic Competence," *Quarterly Journal of Political Science* 5: 193–208.

Hibbing, John R, and Theiss-Morse, Elizabeth. 2002. *Stealth Democracy*. Cambridge University Press.

Hill, Lisa. 2002. "On the Reasonableness of Compelling Citizens to 'Vote': The Australian Case," *Political Studies* 50: 80–101.

Huemer, Michael. 2013. *The Problem of Political Authority*. New York: Palgrave MacMillan.

Inglehart, Ronald, and Hans Klingemann. 1976. "Party Identification, Ideological Preference, and the Left-Right Dimension among Western Mass Publics." In Ian Budge, Ivor Crewe, and Dennis Fairlie, eds., *Party Identification and Beyond*. London: Wiley, 243–73.

Iyengar, Shanto, Sood, Guarav, and Yphtach Lelkes. 2012. "Affect, Not Ideology: A Social Identity Perspective on Polarization," *Public Opinion Quarterly* 76: 405–431.

Iyengar, Shanto, and Sean J. Westwood. 2015. "Fear and Loathing across Party Lines: New Evidence on Group Polarization," *American Journal of Political Science* 59: 690–707.

Jardina, Ashley. 2019. *White Identity Politics*. New York: Cambridge University Press.

Jones, Garrett. 2020. *10% Less Democracy*. Stanford: Stanford University Press.

Kahan, Dan. 2016. "The Politically Motivated Reasoning Paradigm, Part 1: What Political Motivated Reasoning Is and How to Measure It." In *Emerging Trends in the Social and Behavioral Sciences: An Interdisciplinary, Searchable, And Linkable Resource*, https://onlinelibrary.wiley.com/doi/abs/10.1002/9781118900772.etrds0417.

Kahan, Dan, Jenkins-Smith, Hank, and Donald Braman. 2011. "Cultural Cognition of Scientific Consensus," Journal of Risk Research 14: 147–174.

Kahan, Dan, Peters, Ellen, Cantrell Dawson, Erica, and Paul Slovic. 2013. "Motivated Numeracy and Enlightened Self-Government," *Behavioral Public Policy* 1: 54–86.

Kerr, N. L., MacCoun, R. J., and G. P. Kramer. 1996. "Bias in Judgment: Comparing Individuals and Groups, *Psychological Review* 103, 687–719.

Kinder, Donald, and Nathan Kalmoe. 2017. *Neither Liberal nor Conservative: Ideological Innocence in the American Public.* Chicago: University of Chicago Press.

Kahneman, Daniel. 2003. "Maps of Bounded Rationality: Psychology for Behavioral Economics," *American Economic Review* 93: 1449–1475.

Kahneman, Daniel, Slovic, Paul, and Amos Tversky. 1982. *Judgment Under Uncertainty.* New York: Cambridge University Press.

Kelly, James Terence. 2012. *Framing Democracy.* Princeton: Princeton University Press.

Landemore, Hélène. 2012. *Democratic Reason.* Princeton: Princeton University Press.

Landemore, Hélène. 2016. "Yes, We Can (Make It Up on Volume): Answers to Critics," *Critical Review* 2016: 184–237.

Landemore, Hélène. 2017. "Inclusive Constitution Making and Religions Rights: Lessons from the Icelandic Experiment," *Journal of Politics* 79: 762–779.

Leeson, Peter. 2016. *Anarchy Unbound: Why Anarchy Works Better than You Think.* New York: Oxford University Press.

Leigh, Andrew. 2009. "Does the World Economy Swing National Elections?" *Oxford Bulletin of Economics and Statistics* 71: 163–181.

Lenz, Gabriel S. 2009. "Learning and Opinion Change, Not Priming: Reconsidering the Priming Hypothesis," *American Journal of Political Science* 53: 821–837.

Lenz, Gabriel S. 2012. *Follow the Leader? How Voters Respond to Politician's Policies and Performance.* Chicago: University of Chicago Press.

Lenz, Gabriel, and Lawson, Chappell. 2008. "Looking the Part: Television Leads Less Informed Citizens to Vote Based on Candidates' Appearance." Unpublished manuscript, Department of Political Science, Massachusetts Institute of Technology, Cambridge, MA.

Lewis-Beck, Michael, Jacoby, William, Norpoth, Helmut, and Herbert Weisberg. 2008. *The American Voter Revisited*. Ann Arbor: University of Michigan Press.

Lippmann, Walter. 1922. *Public Opinion*. New York: Penguin.

Lodge, Milton, and Charles Taber. 2013. *The Rationalizing Voter*. New York: Cambridge University Press.

López-Guerra, Claudio. 2011. "The Enfranchisement Lottery," *Politics, Philosophy, and Economics* 10: 211–233.

Lupia, Arthur, and Matthew McCubbins. 1998. *The Democratic Dilemma: Can Citizens Learn What They Need To Know?* Cambridge: Cambridge University Press.

Manin, Bernard. 1995. *Principles of Representative Government*. New York: Cambridge University Press.

Marsden, Nancy. 1987. "Note: Gender Dynamics and Jury Deliberations," *Yale Law Journal* 96: 593–612.

Mason, Lilliana. 2017. *Uncivil Agreement: How Politics Became Our Identity*. Chicago: University of Chicago Press.

Mason, Lilliana. 2018. "Ideologues without Issues: The Polarizing Consequences of Ideological Identities," *Public Opinion Quarterly* 82: 280–301.

Mason, Lilliana, and Julie Wronski. 2018. "One Tribe to Bind Them All: How Our Social Group Attachments Strengthen Partisanship," *Political Psychology* 39: 257–277.

McCann, James A. 1997. "Electoral Choices and Core Value Change: The 1992 Presidential Campaign," *American Journal of Political Science* 41: 564–583.

McCarty, Nolan. 2019. *Polarization: What Everyone Needs to Know*. New York: Oxford University Press.

Mendelberg, Tali. 2002. "The Deliberative Citizen: Theory and Evidence." In Michael X. Delli Carpini, Leonie Huddy, and Robert Y. Shapiro, eds., *Research in Micropolitics, Volume 6: Political Decision Making, Deliberation, and Participation*. Amsterdam: Elsevier, 151–193.

Muddle, Case. 2007. "The Single-Issue Party Thesis: Extreme Right Parties and the Immigration Issue," *West European Politics* 22: 182–197.

Mueller, Dennis. 2003. *Public Choice III*. Cambridge: Cambridge University Press.

Mutz, Diana. 2006. *Hearing the Other Side*. Cambridge: Cambridge University Press.

Mutz, Diana. 2008. "Is Deliberative Democracy a Falsifiable Theory?" *Annual Review of Political Science* 11: 521–538.

Myers, C. Daniel, and Tali Mendelberg. 2013. "Political Deliberation." In Leonie Huddy, David Sears, and Jack Levy, eds., *The Oxford Handbook of Political Psychology*. New York: Oxford University Press, 699–734.

Neuman, W. Russell. 1986. *The Paradox of Mass Politics*. Cambridge, MA: Harvard University Press.

Noel, Hans. 2010. "Ten Things Political Scientists Know that You Don't," *The Forum* 8: 1–19.

Nozick, Robert. 1974. *Anarchy, State, and Utopia*. New York: Basic Books.

Önnudóttir, Eva, and Ólafur Harðarson. 2018. "Political Cleavages, Party Voter Linkages and the Impact of Voters' Socio-Economic Status on Vote-Choice in Iceland, 1983–2016/17," *Veftímaritið Stjórnmál og Stjórnsýsla* 14: 101–130.

Oppenheimer, Danny, and Mike Edwards. 2012. *Democracy Despite Itself: Why a System that Shouldn't Work at All Works so Well*. Cambridge, MA: MIT Press.

Ostrom, Elinor. 1990. *Governing the Commons*. New York: Cambridge University Press.

Page, Scott, and Lu Hong. 2004. "Problem Solving by Heterogeneous Agents," *Journal of Economic Theory* 97: 123–163.

Palfrey, Thomas, and Keith Poole. 1987. "The Relationship between Information, Ideology, and Voting Behavior," *American Journal of Political Science* 31: 510–530.

Quirk, Paul J. 2014. "Making It Up on Volume: Are Larger Groups Really Smarter?" *Critical Review* 26: 129–150.

Rasinki, Kenneth A. 1989. "The Effect on Question Wording on Public Support for Government Spending," *Public Opinion Quarterly* 53: 388–394.

Rawls, John. 1971. *A Theory of Justice*. Cambridge: Harvard University Press.

Ryfe, David. 2005. "Does Deliberative Democracy Work?" *Annual Review of Political Science* 8: 49–71.

Schmidtz, David. 1994. "The Institution of Property," *Social Philosophy and Policy* 11: 42–62.

Schwartzberg, Melissa, 2015. "Epistemic Democracy and Its Challenges," *Annual Review of Political Science* 18: 187–203.

Simler, Kevin and Robin Hanson. 2018. *The Elephant in the Brain*. Oxford University Press.

Somin, Ilya. 1998. "Voter Ignorance and the Democratic Ideal," *Critical Review* 12: 413–458.

Somin, Ilya. 2013. *Democracy and Political Ignorance*. Stanford: Stanford University Press.

Stokes, Susan C. 1988. "Pathologies of Deliberation." In John Elster, ed., *Deliberative Democracy*. New York: Cambridge University Press, 123–139.

Stringham, Edward. 2014. *Private Governance*. New York: Oxford University Press.

Sunstein, Cass R. 2002. "The Law of Group Polarization," *Journal of Political Philosophy* 10: 175–195.

Surprenant, Christopher, and Jason Brennan. 2020. *Injustice for All*. New York: Routledge.

Taber, Charles, and Milton R. Lodge. 2006. "Motivated Skepticism in the Evaluation of Political Beliefs," *American Journal of Political Science* 50: 755–769.

Taber, Charles, and Everett Young. 2013. "Political Information Processing." In Leonie Huddy, David Sears, and Jack Levy, eds., *The Oxford Handbook of Political Psychology*. New York: Oxford University Press, 525–558.

Tajfel, Henry. 1981. *Human Groups and Social Categories*. New York: Cambridge University Press.

Tajfel, Henri. 1982. *Social Identity and Intergroup Relations*. Cambridge: Cambridge University Press.

Tajfel, Henry, and J. C. Turner. 1979. "An Integrative Theory of Intergroup Conflict." In W. G. Austin and S. Worchel, eds., *The Social Psychology of Intergroup Relations*. Monterey, CA: Brooks-Cole, 33–37.

Thompson, Abigail. 2014. "Does Diversity Trump Ability?" *Notices of the AMS* 69, 1024–1031.

Todorov, Alexander, Mandisodza, Anesu N., Goren, Amir, and Crystal C. Hall. 2005. "Inferences of Competence from Faces Predict Election Outcomes," *Science* 308: 1623–1626.

Tversky, Andrew, and Daniel Kahneman. 1973. "Availability: A Heuristic for Judging Frequency and Probability," *Cognitive Psychology* 5: 207–233.

Weiner, Greg. 2012. *Madison's Metronome*. Lawrence: University of Kansas Press.

Westen, Drew. 2008. *The Political Brain*. New York: Perseus Books.

Westen, Drew, Pavel S. Blagov, Keith Harenski, Clint Kilts, and Stephan Hamann. 2006. "The Neural Basis of Motivated Reasoning: An fMRI Study of Emotional Constraints on Political Judgment during the US Presidential Election of 2004," *The Journal of Cognitive Neuroscience* 18: 1947–1958.

Zechmeister, Elizabeth. 2006. "What's Left and Who's Right? A Q-method Study of Individual and Contextual Influences on the Meaning of Ideological Labels," *Political Behavior* 28: 151–173.

Zaller, John. 1992. *The Nature and Origins of Mass Opinion*. New York: Cambridge University Press.

Part 2

LANDEMORE—LET'S TRY

REAL DEMOCRACY

Let's Try Real Democracy

The real argument for democracy is, then, that in the people
we have the source of that endless life and unbounded wisdom
which the rulers of men must have.

—W. E. B. DU BOIS, *On the Ruling of Men*, p. 84

INTRODUCTION

"The best argument against democracy is a five-minute conversation with the average voter." This oft-repeated quip by Churchill captures the essence of nearly all attacks on democracy, recent or past. Jason Brennan builds his case against democracy on the empirical claims of the behavioral literature of the last forty years concerning the alleged incompetence of the average voter. Similarly, Daniel Bell, an advocate of China's hierarchical, meritocratic model, justifies his preference for rule by "knowers" on the basis of voter ignorance observed in the US and speculated in the case of China.[1] Self-proclaimed democrats themselves

1. "Based on solid empirical evidence . . . , I argue that the quality of voters is also low in countries such as the United States, and there is no reason to believe that Chinese voters will become any more rational or public-spirited than voters anywhere else" (Bell 2015, xi).

Debating Democracy. Jason Brennan and Hélène Landemore, Oxford University Press. © Oxford University Press 2022. DOI: 10.1093/oso/9780197540817.003.0006

sometimes use these empirical findings to justify lowering our normative expectations as to the meaning of democracy. In *Democracy for Realists*, for example, Chris Achen and Larry Bartels urge that, in light of the available evidence, we should give up on the ideal of democracy as a regime based on popular judgment and responsive to the wishes of the majority. They suggest settling instead for the Schumpeterian vision of democracy as a regime in which elites compete for uninformed, irrational, biased, and identity-driven votes and where the only point of elections is to send random shocks to the system, thereby preventing the worst of elite domination (Schumpeter 1942). Unlike the arguments by Brennan or Bell, these democratic "realists" do not send us straight into the arms of technocrats and experts, but their pessimistic outlook is hardly a source of comfort. With friends like these . . .

Antidemocratic views are, in fact, all around us. On January 1, 2017, *The New Yorker* published a cartoon of ambiguous political humor that presumably resonated with many readers, even as it explicitly undermined foundational democratic beliefs. The cartoon shows a man standing inside the economy cabin of a plane, addressing his fellow passengers this way: "These smug pilots have lost touch with regular passengers like us. Who thinks I should fly the plane?" All the passengers, including himself, raise their hands.

The cartoon was published on the heels of the American presidential election that brought Donald Trump to power. It can be read as a denunciation of populism, wherein an incompetent nobody can claim a right to rule the polity instead of those whom the same incompetent nobody denounces as corrupt and out-of-touch elites. The cartoon also lampoons the populist's desire to bypass the representative structures of government and take matters into their own hands, despite having no training, expertise, or experience. Both ideas—the choice of a populist leader and the ideal of direct self-rule—are presented as being as stupid as having the passengers of a plane take command over professional pilots. Thus, on the face of it, the cartoon mocks rule by ordinary citizens while at the same time endorsing another alternative, namely, the rule of experts—what I will refer to as "epistocracy," or the "rule of the knowers."[2]

The metaphor used in the cartoon—politics as a plane in need of expert pilots—is straightforwardly Platonic in spirit. Plato famously compared politics to a ship that can only be steered by the people with the relevant knowledge and expertise (the philosophers). The metaphor of politics as ship-steering (or plane-piloting) is profoundly elitist in its assumptions of who, in politics, has legitimate authority. Unsurprisingly, democrats of Plato's time rejected it. The Sophist Protagoras, for example, argued against Socrates, who stands for Plato on this topic in the eponymous dialogue, that politics was precisely *not* like ship-steering, or ship-building, or any other technical realm of life. Politics was, instead, for Protagoras, about living well together, in other words, the common good, about which all of us have

2. David Estlund (1997, 2008) has coined and popularized the term "epistocracy," after the Greek word for knowledge, *episteme*, cut short by one syllable (apparently for concision's sake). While I still think "epistemocracy" would have been a more etymologically correct neologism, I will use here the term he popularized, namely "epistocracy."

the ability, and the right, to say something. It is for this reason, Protagoras proudly notes, that while amateurs are booed into silence in the Assembly when it comes to technical questions, on matters of the public good, by contrast, Athenians have an equal right of speech ("*isegoria*").

If it is true, as Athenian democrats believed, that in politics we all deserve a say, then *The New Yorker* cartoon is deeply problematic. Politics is about where we are going as a group and, perhaps, whether we should go there by boat or by plane. It is only secondarily, though importantly, about choosing the pilots who should take us where we want to go. Even the implicit analogy between political leaders and ship captains or plane pilots is wrong since leadership is less about expert knowledge than moral vision. Political leadership is not just about being able to maneuver the ship or fly the plane; it is, more importantly, about being able to pick the right direction. If we must compare someone with pilots, it should be experts and bureaucrats, not necessarily democratic representatives or leaders.

Critics like Brennan and Bell argue that ordinary citizens lack the requisite knowledge even to choose the right direction. Some democrats might be inclined to concede this point and to defend democracy on other grounds. However, there is a long tradition of authors who have argued for democracy not despite knowledge-based (or "epistemic") considerations, but precisely because of them. The argument is that the knowledge necessary to govern well comes from the people themselves and that democratic procedures are required to access such knowledge. The history of epistemic arguments for democracy goes from Protagoras to modern "epistemic democrats" (including myself) through, among others, Aristotle, Machiavelli, Condorcet, John Stuart Mill, and W. E. B. Du Bois. Du Bois offers what is probably the most inspiring version of the argument, which is why I chose a quotation of his as an epigraph to this essay.

The arguments put forward by the members of this long tradition have not satisfied democracy's challengers, however. Even 2500 years after Protagoras, we are still debating the relative merits of democracy and oligarchic regimes like China and Singapore. In this debate, I will argue the side of the Sophist, against Socrates and Plato— not an easy task, especially given the crisis of democracy widely diagnosed in recent decades. My argument, however, will lead us to what is perhaps a surprising thought. If the regimes we call democracies fail to deliver the good governance that epistemic arguments predict they should deliver, it could be that these regimes are insufficiently democratic to begin with, in that they are not sufficiently empowering and inclusive of their citizens. As a result, not only do these regimes questionably deserve the title of democracy, they are also bound to suffer from epistemic limitations. That is why, ultimately, I support institutional reforms to get closer to the ideal of people's power, building on a non-electoral model of democracy that I call "open democracy."

In chapter five, I lay out a general theoretical case for democracy, specifically the kind of democracy that democratic theorists call "deliberative democracy," which traces the legitimacy of laws and policies to the reasoned exchange of arguments among free and equal citizens.

I show the benefits of distributing political decision-power in an inclusive and egalitarian manner, especially in the deliberative phase of the legislative process. The core idea is that many minds deliberating together are better than few when it comes to dealing with the uncertainty and complexity of the world and figuring out solutions that work for all within it.

In chapter six, I address theoretical and empirical objections that critics have presented against my argument, which I call the argument from collective wisdom. The objections I address include those based on the average voter's alleged incompetence and systematic biases, as well as those that challenge the relevance of deductive arguments for democracy.

In chapter seven, I argue against both oligarchic and majoritarian rule by knowers, that is different varieties of so-called "epistocracies." Such regimes are necessarily blind to certain interests and perspectives, rendering them epistemically inferior to authentic edemocracies over the long term.

In chapter eight, I return to the ideal of people's power and argue that democracies as we know them are dubiously democratic. Most ordinary citizens, in the US certainly but in other so-called "democracies" as well, have little deliberative input into and influence over the laws and policies that rule their lives. I trace the problem to fundamental design mistakes made in the eighteenth century when elections, an oligarchic selection mechanism, rather than the traditional lot of Classical Athens, were identified as the proper method for choosing representatives. This fundamental design mistake explains in part why contemporary democracies are, and indeed have always been, dysfunctional. Therefore I, like Brennan, argue that we can do better than so-called "representative democracy." But my answer will be to grant more power to ordinary citizens. In short, I propose more democracy, not less. I then make a case for a new paradigm of democracy that I call "open democracy," which takes more seriously the core ideal of people's power and, somewhat provocatively, does away with elected assemblies. Even though actual reform plans should more reasonably seek to hybridize our electoral systems with lottery-based citizen participation, it is useful, at a theoretical level, to imagine an entirely non-electoral open democracy.

Chapter 5

The Argument
for Democracy

IN WHAT FOLLOWS, I PRESENT A deductive argument for democracy, based on some assumptions about the nature of democratic procedures and the conditions under which they operate. I offer here a condensed version of the argument that I have developed more extensively elsewhere.

The epistemic argument for democracy presented here is a version of the argument from "the wisdom of the multitude" (Waldron 1995) that can be traced back to the ancient Sophists and that Aristotle first analyzed as the claim that "many heads are better than one" (*Politics* 3.11). In recent years, works done in philosophy (e.g., Anderson 2006, Estlund 2008) and political science (e.g., Ober 2008; Goodin and Spiekermann 2019) have taken up the epistemic argument in modernized forms (see also Landemore 2021 for a survey).

In the version I propose here (building on Landemore 2012, 2013, and 2021), democracy is modeled as a collective decision procedure involving the combination of two mechanisms: inclusive and egalitarian deliberation on the one hand and simple majority rule combined with universal

Debating Democracy. Jason Brennan and Hélène Landemore, Oxford University Press. © Oxford University Press 2022. DOI: 10.1093/oso/9780197540817.003.0007

suffrage on the other. This procedure operates under the conditions of politics in general—namely, the pursuit of the common good under conditions of uncertainty. I argue that when it comes to producing good results for the members of the relevant group, democratic decision procedures are superior to all other pure decision rules that grant decision-making power to one person or a few people instead of the many. I assume that all participants in these decision-making scenarios pursue the common good and are equipped with the same competent bureaucracies so as not to bias the comparison in favor of one regime or another from the start. If all decision rules compete under the same conditions, with the only difference between them being how many people's voices they include, which one comes out on top over the long run?

My claim is that democracy does better than less inclusive and less egalitarian decision rules because, by including all voices equally, it structurally maximizes the cognitive diversity brought to bear on collective problems. Cognitive diversity is defined here as the difference between each one of us in terms of the ways we see problems and make predictions about future outcomes, based on the different models we intuitively develop about the way the world works or should be interpreted. Cognitive diversity is distinct from both its symptoms (a different set of viewpoints or opinions) and its possible root causes (e.g., gender or ethnic diversity) as well as a diversity that can actually be epistemically harmful, namely a diversity of fundamental goals or values. [1] That there exists something like cognitive

1. In an epistemic framework, all the members of the group are supposed to pursue the same goal and want the same

diversity among human beings is rendered plausible by the fact that individuals come equipped with different cognitive toolboxes (see theories of "multiple intelligence," e.g., Gardner 1983; Sternberg 1985; Salovey and Mayer 1990). The specificity of individual cognitive processes is a property that is determined by multiple factors, from genetic makeup to cultural factors and life experiences, and can thus vary greatly from one individual to the next, and may even vary for the same individual over his lifetime. Cognitive differences thus need not be hard-wired. People may just have different models about the world because of where they stand geographically in it.

Cognitive diversity thus defined is a group property that has been shown to be a crucial factor of group performance in various contexts. In fact, under certain conditions, cognitive diversity turns out to be more important for the problem-solving abilities of a group than does the average competence of its members (Page 2007, 163). This surprising result turns on its head the received wisdom that group competence is merely a function of individual competence, or that, in other words, the more we staff our decision-making group with "the best and brightest," the smarter the group will be. It turns out that such a strategy will often be less successful than a strategy that consists

thing, namely to find the right answer or make an accurate prediction. This is a bit of an oversimplification since for any given fundamental common goal or value (e.g., economic growth, public health, national security, the preservation of the environment etc.), the problem-solving aspect can accommodate, and even benefit from, less fundamental value diversity (e.g., between a Keynesian and an Austrian economist).

of simply aiming for a high enough level of individual competence while maximizing the cognitive diversity of the group along the relevant lines.

I argue that under the conditions of uncertainty that characterize politics in general, decision-making characterized by maximal inclusiveness and equality is correlated with greater cognitive diversity, which in turn is correlated with better problem-solving and prediction.

If the goal is to compose an all-purpose assembly of democratic representatives, my argument implies that a good strategy is to take a random sample of the larger population and form a statistically representative mini. This argument assumes that on average citizens are at least competent enough to engage in a deliberation about political issues. (Landemore 2012; 2013). At the end of this essay, I return to the role of randomly selected representatives in the reformed version of democracy that I call "open democracy."

This argument from the collective intelligence of the people, as harnessed by deliberative, inclusive, and egalitarian decision procedures, applies primarily to democratic assemblies. It can apply to the smallest of directly democratic assemblies (a group of friends choosing a restaurant) and to all types of representative assemblies, from the local to the national, federal, and global levels.[2]

---

2. The argument could, in theory, be extended to referenda or any judgment aggregation in a large group provided one can give a convincing account of epistemically sound mass deliberation preceding the voting phase (a task I will not attempt here but see Parkinson and Mansbridge 2012 for an attempt among advocates of the so-called systemic turn in deliberative democracy).

To the extent that the regimes we call democracies are primarily centered around such representative assemblies, the argument applies to these regime forms as well, though I am more cautious regarding this macro-claim, which remains conjectural at this point. Empirical evidence would have to demonstrate that the positive outcomes we associate with existing "democratic" regimes are caused by the democratic features of inclusive and egalitarian deliberation within assemblies (a tall order given the many confounding factors at that level of analysis).[3]

The epistemic argument suggests that we would be better off under a model of what I call "open democracy" than under any epistocracy and even electoral democracy. "Open democracy" is a non-electoral form of representative democracy centered around a randomly selected legislative assembly itself connected to a network of other randomly selected assemblies at the local level. Finally, the epistemic argument translates to other environments that we are not used to seeing as political, such as firms, the universites, hospitals, even the army, were they to ever consider making decisions through democratic representative assemblies, whether electoral or "open." Extending the argument to such sites, however, is beyond the purview of this essay.

3. In the same cautious vein, I consider it plausible that democracies can also epistemically benefit from a combination of deliberation among democratic representatives (whether elected or randomly selected) followed by a nationwide referendum, provided that the conclusions of the small group of deliberators have been properly disseminated in and discussed by the larger population prior to the voting moment. See also Landemore 2018.

To reiterate the usefulness of an epistemic argument for democracy, recall that many people justify democracy on non-instrumental grounds by appealing to principles like autonomy, freedom, and political equality. But what could convince someone not already committed to such values, or left unmoved by appeals to fundamental moral claims of the kind that intrinsic arguments tend to rely on, that they should embrace democratic procedures like inclusive deliberation or majority rule? Such persons are unlikely to be convinced, in particular, by the claim that inclusive deliberation and majority rule best express the equality of citizens since the desirability of political equality is precisely the point of contention.

The most obvious and indeed the only alternative is an instrumental argument of the following type: If we include everyone in the deliberation process and count people's votes equally, we are more likely to produce good outcomes (see also Knight and Johnson 2011). The epistemic argument is just one variant of such an instrumental case, specifically emphasizing the knowledge-aggregating and truth-tracking properties of decision procedures that reflect the principle of political equality. Note that the epistemic argument is meant to complement and buttress intrinsic justifications for democracy, rather than replace them or compete with them.[4]

Let me now turn to the two main epistemic engines of democracy: inclusive and egalitarian deliberation and majority rule with universal suffrage.

4. See Landemore 2015, 192–195 for more on the relation between intrinsic and instrumental arguments for democracy.

THE EPISTEMIC PROPERTIES
OF DEMOCRATIC DELIBERATION

In my model, the central mechanism that produces the epistemic properties of democracy is inclusive and egalitarian deliberation.

What reasons do we have to believe that democratic deliberation, understood as an inclusive and egalitarian way of arriving at collective decisions, has epistemic properties—that is, the ability to aggregate the relevant knowledge and track the best possible answers to collective problems?

Deliberation means, roughly, the pondering and weighing of reasons or exchange of arguments for or against a given view. In this sense, deliberation can refer to an internal dialogue in the vein of "deliberation within" (Goodin 2005), an intersubjective exercise among individuals, or a reasoned exchange occurring among entities larger than individuals, as in system-thinking (Parkinson and Mansbridge 2012).

The idea that intersubjective deliberation (leaving aside anything about "democratic" deliberation for the moment) has epistemic properties is an old one. It can arguably be traced back to Aristotle's idea that "many heads are better than one" and to Mill's emphasis on diversity of points of view in helping the truth overcome falsities in a free market of ideas. An underlying assumption of these views is that the truth has a self-revealing nature, which when made apparent through the exchange of viewpoints is supposed to convince all participants in the deliberation (if not instantaneously then over time, and if not inexorably then at least under favorable conditions). This is something best expressed, perhaps, by Habermas's idea of the "unforced force of the better argument" (Habermas 1996). Note that this assumption—sometimes called "the oracle" assumption—is only required for deliberation to become conclusive, that is, to land participants on a single, correct answer. In most real-life cases, however, the best we can probably hope for is to reduce the range of options to the two most plausible ones, leaving it to a vote to settle the disagreement between participants.

How does this "unforced force of the better argument" work in practice, when it works? Let us look at the way deliberation functions in a nicely idealized (but not *too* idealized) model: the deliberations of jurors in the 1957 film *12 Angry Men* by Sidney Lumet.

One of the turning points in the deliberation comes when Juror 8 produces a copy of the murder weapon, a cheap switchblade that he said he was able to buy for a fistful of dollars around the corner from the court, disproving at once the unusualness and identifying nature of the weapon. Another argument is produced by Juror 5, who grew up in a violent slum and can explain the proper way of using a switchblade, raising doubts in the process about the plausibility of the eyewitness's description. The eyewitness's reliability is further put in doubt when it becomes clear that she usually wears glasses (as evidenced by red marks on the side of her nose observed by the jurors when she came to testify). Ultimately a unanimous consensus emerges that the young man should be found not guilty.

The story illustrates the epistemic properties of deliberation. First, it allows participants to weed out the good arguments, interpretations, and information from the bad ones (e.g., the switchblade is not as unique a weapon as previously thought and can only be used a certain way). Second, deliberative problem-solving can also produce synergies, that is, create new solutions out of the arguments, information, and solutions brought to the table (e.g., making sense of the red marks on the eyewitness's nose in a way that proves decisive to the interpretation of her reliability). Third, hearing the perspectives of others may entirely reshape a person's view of the problem and introduce possibilities not initially considered (e.g., the eyewitness testimony cannot be trusted after all). Finally, in the ideal, deliberation produces a unanimous consensus on the "right" solution ("not guilty" in this case).

The example also illustrates the specific merit of deliberation among a diverse group of people. In the story all twelve jurors mattered, in all their differences, because it is only through the interplay between their conflicting interpretations of the evidence and arguments, shaped by each juror's personal history, socioeconomic background, type of intelligence, and so on, that something like the truth ultimately emerges. The epistemic properties of deliberation become manifest despite the fact that the protagonists are far from ideal human beings: one juror just wants to be done with the deliberation and go to a baseball game, one is a bigoted racist, and another is biased by irrelevant fatherly emotions. Deliberation, in other words, can overcome several moral and cognitive limitations.

Lu Hong and Scott Page's Diversity Trumps Ability Theorem encapsulates the epistemic logic of deliberation. It states that under certain conditions "a randomly selected collection of problem solvers outperforms a collection of the best individual problem solvers" (Hong and Page 2004, 16388; Page 2007, 163).[5] In other words, "diversity trumps ability" and our twelve angry men are better than twelve clones of, say, Juror number 8 (arguably the smartest of the lot) would have been. Diversity here refers to *cognitive* diversity, which, as defined earlier, is roughly the difference in the ways that different people will think about a problem in the world. The four conditions for the theorem to hold are (1) that the problem in question is difficult enough; (2) all problem-solvers need to be relatively smart or "not too dumb"; (3) problem-solvers should think differently from each other but should still be able to recognize the best solution; and finally (4) the population from which problem-solvers are selected should be large and the group of problem-solvers should not be too small (Landemore 2013, 102; Page 2007, 163).[6]

Note that the epistemic logic at work in problem-solving among cognitively diverse groups is distinct from the statistical logic behind the Condorcet Jury Theorem, the Miracle of Aggregation, or Hong and Page's other results, the Diversity Prediction Theorem and the Crowd

---

5. For a discussion of the theorem and its application to political science (and the real world more generally), see critics such as Quirk 2014; Thompson 2014; Brennan 2016,182. For the defenders, see Landemore 2014b, 2015; Kuehn 2017; Singer 2019; Sakai 2020.
6. Whether or not these four conditions all translate neatly to the real world of politics and democratic citizens is a contested issue. See Anderson 2006 and Landemore 2013 for application to the democratic context.

Beats Average Law (more on that in next section). *The delib-erative logic has nothing to do with the law of large numbers.* The point here is not that a clear signal will emerge out of the noise of random errors that cancel out, even though the good and bad input alike get aggregated. It is that delib-eration will weed out the bad information and arguments from the outcome entirely.

While the arguments above may account for the epis-temic properties of deliberation among cognitively diverse people, they do not quite justify *democratic* deliberation. Democratic deliberation is often understood as intersub-jective deliberation that takes place specifically in a pub-lic manner among free and equal individuals and is also inclusive of the entirety of the relevant group. However, this definition is generally left implicit in most scholarship on deliberative democracy.

Deliberation thus requires publicity of the discursive exchanges, full inclusiveness, and equal standing and equal opportunities for participation among participants in order to count as plausibly democratic. Theorists appre-ciative of the epistemic value of deliberation may not nec-essarily see the epistemic value of *democratic* deliberation thus understood. After all, Mill, who is often accepted as a deliberative democrat, was also an advocate of a plural vot-ing scheme that gave more voice (in the form of votes) to the learned and was also deeply skeptical of the uneducated person's ability to run for office. Clearly one can believe in the value of deliberation and not think that all involved should have an equal right to be heard.

Here is what I believe to be the missing link between the epistemic properties of deliberation and the epistemic properties of specifically *democratic* deliberation.[7] *More inclusive assemblies are more likely to be cognitively diverse.* To the extent that cognitive diversity is a crucial ingredient of collective intelligence, and specifically one that matters more than average individual ability, the more inclusive the deliberation process is, the smarter the solutions resulting from it should be, overall. Numbers, in other words, function as a proxy for cognitive diversity. This is the gist of my "Numbers Trump Ability Theorem" (Landemore 2013, 104), which modifies the aforementioned "Diversity Trumps Ability Theorem."

To quote from my past work:

> The second step of my argument—my addendum to Page and Hong—proposes that the "cheapest" (i.e., easiest and most economical) way to achieve cognitive diversity in the absence of knowledge about the nature of complex and ever-changing political problems is to include everyone in the group. My argument here is that including everyone is the only way to get all the perspectives, heuristics, interpretations, predictive models, and information that may matter at some point (although you do not know in advance when) . . . This "Numbers Trump Ability Theorem" thus supports a strong epistemic case for democracy, in which my key innovation is to support inclusiveness for its instrumental, specifically epistemic properties: Under the right conditions, including everyone in the decision-making process simply

7. At least when it comes to the inclusive and egalitarian features of the latter, as the publicity element has yet to be shown to have epistemic properties of its own.

makes the group more likely to get the right (or, at least better) answers (Landemore 2014a, 188).

In other words, under conditions of uncertainty, which I argue are central to politics, the best proxy for cognitive diversity is full inclusiveness (i.e., numbers). Where full inclusiveness proves unfeasible,[8] representation by random selection is the next best solution.

MAJORITY RULE WITH UNIVERSAL SUFFRAGE

Deliberation is far from being a perfect or complete decision mechanism, in part because it is time-consuming and rarely produces unanimity (the "oracle" assumption does not always hold). In most cases, it needs to be supplemented by another decision procedure: majority rule utilized to resolve the disagreements among the people who have previously deliberated. Majority rule among a wider group, as in the case of a referendum, raises new issues, since not all the members of the larger group may be aware of the reasons exchanged among the smaller group. A free-standing (weaker) epistemic defense of referenda can, however, be built on the mathematical results that support the epistemic properties of pure judgment aggregation, as I will now present. Nevertheless, the epistemic merits of large-scale judgment aggregation are going to be heavily dependent on the quality of the society-wide public debates taking place (or

8. For practical reasons having to do with the unfeasibility of proper, legitimacy-granting deliberation at scale.

failing to take place) before the moment of voting; for example, via something like Ackerman and Fishkin's imagined Deliberation Day or something like the recent and actual French Great National Debate.

While majority rule is more efficient time-wise than deliberation, it cannot itself generate solutions to problems. It allows, however, for choosing between pre-determined options that have ideally been defined in a deliberation process. Far from simply being a fair way to settle disagreement about the choice of an option, majority rule is also a reliable way to improve the chances of the group picking the right one (where the "right" one can simply be the better one compared to the other options). Majority rule aggregates individuals' judgments about the best course of action to take or the right candidate to elect. In other words, majority rule is not only a fair way to settle on a decision when time is running out for deliberation, but a way to turn imperfect individual predictions into accurate collective ones. Again, since majority rule is available to the lone tyrant, who is the majority by himself, and a group of oligarchs, we need to consider whether majority rule under universal suffrage is superior to majority rule used by a minority within the larger group (it is not). There exist at least three related but distinct theoretical arguments for the epistemic properties of majority rule: the Condorcet Jury Theorem, the Miracle of Aggregation, and Scott Page's "The Crowd Beats the Average Law." All of them add up to an argument for the epistemic properties of majority rule under universal suffrage; that is, for decisions made by the larger rather than the smaller group, based on one person, one vote.

The CJT demonstrates that among large electorates voting on some binary (yes or no) question, majoritarian outcomes are virtually certain to track the "truth," as long as three conditions hold: (1) voters are better than random at choosing true propositions; (2) they vote independently of each other; and (3) they vote sincerely or truthfully. The Miracle of Aggregation is an account of the statistical phenomenon by which a few informed people in a group are enough to guide the group to the right average answer, as long as the mean of uninformed people's answers is zero.[9] Here, collective intelligence depends on extracting the information held by an informed elite from the mass of noise represented by other people's opinions. As long as a sizeable minority in the crowd (the minority needs to be pivotal) knows the right answer and everyone else makes mistakes that cancel each other out, the right answer is still going to rise to the surface. The classic example illustrating the Miracle of Aggregation is the weight-guessing game observed by the nineteenth-century statistician Francis Galton at a country fair, in which the average answer of 800 participants' guesses regarding the weight of an ox once slaughtered and dressed turned out to fall within one pound of the right answer.[10] Galton is said to have been prompted by this result to compare the guessing game with democratic voting and to conclude that "[t]he result seems more creditable to the trustworthiness of democratic judgment than might have been expected" (Galton 1907, 246). Note that the miracle occurs at the level of aggregated

---

9. This version probably goes back to Berelson, Lazarsfeld, and McPhee (1954).
10. Many other anecdotes, recounted in both Surowiecki (2004) and Sunstein (2006), vividly illustrate the same "miracle" of group intelligence.

judgments about some quantifiable value—e.g., the weight of an ox—for which people's guesses will be different discrete values. In the case of majority rule, where we assume that the answer is yes or no as opposed to such quantitative values, the aggregated judgment is whatever answer— yes or no, left or right—gets at least $(n/2)+1$ votes. If we assume that only one person in the crowd knows the right answer and the others randomize their choice, the miracle will occur only if the person with the right answer is also pivotal. As n grows large, we need to assume that at least a sizable minority knows the right answer—sizable enough to have better-than-random chances of being pivotal—or, as in the Condorcet Jury Theorem, that everyone in the group has at least a slightly better than random chance of knowing the right answer.

Both the Condorcet Jury Theorem[11] and the Miracle of Aggregation[12] are versions of the Law of Large Numbers, meaning that the epistemic properties of judgment aggregation only manifest with certainty at the limit for an infinity of voters (provided the relevant conditions are met).

11. First formulated by the Marquis de Condorcet at the end of the eighteenth century (Condorcet 1785), the CJT was rediscovered by Duncan Black in the 1950s. Since then, it has spawned many formal analyses (e.g., to name a few, Grofman, Owen, and Feld 1983; Lhada 1992; List and Goodin 2001; and Bovens and Rabinowicz 2006) and been the subject of a book-length study (Goodin and Spiekerman 2018). I refer the reader to these sources for an in-depth exploration.
12. E.g., Converse 1990; Page and Shapiro 1992; Wittman 1995; Caplan 2007.

Given this limitation, I want to focus instead on the account offered by Lu Hong and Scott Page, which is based not on the Law of Large Numbers but on models of cognitive diversity. In a series of co-authored articles and a book (Hong and Page 2001; 2004; 2009; Page 2007), Lu Hong and Scott Page propose a different account of why large groups of people can make good judgments and, in particular, accurate predictions. Although Hong and Page's model generally applies to numerical predictions that are not of a binary form (e.g., predicting sales figures), it can also apply to scenarios in which judgments are binary (e.g., predicting whether a candidate is competent or incompetent). In my view, Hong and Page's model can explicate majority rule's epistemic properties.

The logic of cognitive diversity in group judgment aggregation is formalized in two mathematical results: the Diversity Prediction Theorem and the Crowd Beats Average Law. The first theorem states that when we average people's predictions, a group's collective error equals the average individual error minus the group members' predictive diversity (Page 2007, 208). In other words, when it comes to predicting outcomes, cognitive differences among the participants matter just as much as individual ability. Increasing predictive diversity by one unit results in the same reduction in collective error as does increasing average ability by one unit.

The second theorem—the Crowd Beats Average Law—states that the accuracy of the group's prediction as determined by the average prediction cannot be worse than the average accuracy of its members. In other words, the group necessarily predicts more accurately than its average member. Further, the amount by which the group "outpredicts" its average member increases as the group becomes more diverse (Page 2007, 197). This law follows directly from the Diversity Prediction Theorem.

What does all of this mean? In order to maximize our chances of picking the better of two options, we are better off, as a group, taking the average (or potentially median) answer of a sufficiently cognitively diverse group of people than letting a randomly selected individual in that group make a choice for the group. This is so because, for a given group of people using different predictive models, the predictions will be negatively correlated and mistakes will cancel each other out not randomly but systematically. Consequently, the average error of the group will be less than the average error of a randomly selected voter. This result holds true to a greater degree as the difference between the predictive models used by the voters increases (i.e., as there is more cognitive diversity in the group).

It might not be immediately apparent how this account of the properties of the average (or median) judgment of a group applies to majority rule, which generally involves yes or no questions where no average is available. Yet, as in the case of the Miracle of Aggregation, the logic of the cognitive diversity account can be extended to such binary answers by turning each option into a quantifiable value (with yes corresponding to the value 1 and no corresponding to the value 0, for example) and seeing the majoritarian result as the closest rounding of the average result. Note that this suggests the superiority of a rating system (like so-called majority judgment) over majority rule per se.

The superiority of Page's account over the CJT or the Miracle of Aggregation, in my view, is at least twofold. First, his account circumvents the problematic assumption of judgment independence, which rendered both the CJT and the Miracle of Aggregation somewhat unrealistic. The independence assumption is now applied, more plausibly, not to people's actual judgments (their outputs) but to the cognitive processes leading to those judgments (i.e., the predictive models that people use to generate judgments and predictions about the world). By internalizing the independence constraint, Page's model opens up the black box of voters' decision-making processes. It also makes it possible for citizens to share information, premises, and even conclusions, while remaining "independent" in terms of the cognitive processes that made use of the shared information and generated the shared conclusions.

The second advantage is that Page's model supports the epistemic reliability of majority rule used among small groups.[13] The emphasis in Page's account is not so much on the existence of a large number of votes as it is on the existence of sufficient cognitive diversity in the group, no matter its size (since cognitive diversity is what ensures that votes (or predictions) are not independent but, on the contrary, negatively correlated to ensure systematic cancellations of individual mistakes). Unlike what happens with the CJT or the Miracle of Aggregation, we do not need to have an infinity of voters for majority rule to guarantee 100% predictive accuracy. Because cognitive diversity can

---

13. In fact, his account is more optimistic for small groups than very large ones. I do not have the space to address this concern here. But it seems to be the case that majority rule used in representative assemblies is more likely to have epistemic properties than majority rule used in referenda.

exist as soon as more than one person is making the pre-diction, the magic can work for a group with as few as three members. The group's performance improves with the addition of a person with a sufficiently different predictive model. In the CJT, by contrast, the major payoff of major-ity rule is only with large numbers; adding one person to the group does not make much of a difference.[14]

Whichever account of the epistemic properties of majority rule is favored—CJT, Miracle of Aggregation, or Cognitive Diversity Models—the conclusion is the same: if their assumptions are verified, the group's prediction, using majority rule, will be epistemically superior to that of the average citizen in the group. These accounts provide an argument in favor of the claim that the rule of the many is superior to the rule of one (when the one is randomly chosen). They do not, however, give us a maximal argu-ment in favor of majority rule since majority rule among the many does not systematically beat majority rule used among a few smart people. It is, therefore, the superiority

---

14. The flip side of this, however, is that in Page's model there is a theoretical limit to the amount that collective judg-ment can be improved by including more and more people. Cognitive diversity in judgment aggregation is not a lin-ear function of numbers and there are in fact diminishing returns to adding more people past a certain point. What the cognitive model suggests here is that it is probably bet-ter to aggregate the views of a limited number of represen-tatives than those of millions of voters. At the scale of an assembly of representatives, aggregating more judgments can be expected to have increasing returns in terms of cognitive diversity, which may be lost when we aggregate the views of millions of citizens.

of democratic deliberation over oligarchic deliberation (as defended in previous section above) that allows us to derive the more ambitious claim for democracy as a combination of deliberation and majority rule.

ASSUMPTIONS

Several assumptions need to be verified for the argument to work. The first is that politics is an uncertain game. By contrast, if the bundle of political issues that any human group faces over time were complex but known, even on a merely probabilistic level, then a credible case could be made that we would be better off weighing more heavily the voices and votes of experts, understood as people with the time and smarts to perform the proper risk assessment. We could identify these experts by looking at the past performance of a given population and figuring out those with the best forecasting records over many years. Giving more voice and votes to such individuals would often mean giving zero weight—that is, no voice and no vote at all—to a vast majority of the population. This is exactly what epistocracy or a Chinese-style meritocracy claim, and also the legitimating basis of systems of plural voting with limited franchise (the partial epistemocracies Brennan wants us to resurrect).

The presence of uncertainty, however, defines an entirely new game. Uncertainty means that we cannot fully anticipate what the future will be like, whether in the short term or the long term, and whether, in particular, it will be sufficiently like the past (the way, say, business cycles may repeat familiar patterns) or different in radically new ways (as when a pandemic, a war, or a climate emergency suddenly complicate familiar political questions in unpredictable ways). As a result, no one person or group of persons can be trusted to have the relevant knowledge or skills that make them the superior decision-makers in every situation, and it becomes rational to follow instead a simple heuristic that distributes power over the entire group: give everyone the same participation rights in the decision-making process. This general heuristic translates further into two sub-heuristics: an equal right to speech and equal vote.

Let me make explicit another key assumption of the reasoning thus far. I assume throughout that the larger population's knowledge is more evenly distributed across all political issues than political experts' knowledge. In other words, I assume that, whereas the knowledge of the larger population tends to spread more or less evenly across all political topics, political experts' knowledge will cluster on certain areas of politics. This point is important because if experts' knowledge were just as evenly distributed across issues as the knowledge of the larger population, then one would have reasons to oppose the equal weighting of all views and to give more weight to the experts (provided they could successfully be identified as such).

This assumption of uneven distribution of experts' knowledge across political issues seems defensible: most political problems have a diversity of geography, class, race, and gender components, whereas "expertness" —at least insofar as it is sociologically traceable—tends to skew urban, wealthy, white, and male. This assumption is also plausible given that only certain political issues are salient in the curriculum and training dispensed by universities and law, business, and journalism schools, where experts acquire their status. It is plausible, finally, based on the fact that this distributive unevenness can be observed outside of politics. Consider, for example, the contrast between Wikipedia and expert-written encyclopedias. Written by amateurs, Wikipedia covers the whole range of human interests (including topics such as "Paris Hilton" and "Game of Thrones"). By contrast, the topics covered by expert-written encyclopedias are comparatively fewer and narrower (more high-brow). Combined with the uncertainty of politics, this difference in knowledge distribution makes it sensible to resist giving the experts, who know a lot about a relatively narrow set of topics, more weight than the rest of the citizens, who know less but cover a much greater variety of topics.

Chapter 6

Objections

LET ME TURN TO TWO kinds of objections that one could make to the argument laid out in the previous chapter. The first kind of objection is empirical, relying on documented evidence of citizen ignorance and systematic biases, which would seem to falsify the claim that ordinary citizens are capable of good deliberation and voting. The other is theoretical, directed to the deductive nature of my argument: some would allege that a deductive argument cannot prove anything of relevance to real-life democracies (or any other regime, for that matter).

OBJECTION ONE: CITIZENS ARE TOO IGNORANT AND SYSTEMATICALLY BIASED FOR DEMOCRACY TO WORK

In *Against Democracy* and the first part of this book, Brennan argues that democracies cannot work optimally because we have indubitable social scientific evidence that voters do not know anything, or do not know enough, or may even know less than nothing, in that they are biased in systematic ways that make them worse as a group than

Debating Democracy. Jason Brennan and Hélène Landemore, Oxford University Press. © Oxford University Press 2022. DOI: 10.1093/oso/9780197540817.003.0008

as individuals. The empirical evidence points to two major problems for democracy:

(1) Voters are politically ignorant, as measured through empirical surveys (observational data) that ask representative samples of citizens to answer questions such as, "What is the name of your senator?" or "What is the capital of Japan?"; and

(2) voters possess systemic biases, revealed as systematic discrepancies between the public's preferences and beliefs on the one hand and those of their better-informed selves on the other. Their better-informed selves are constructed as either a simulated public statistically endowed with the knowledge of facts deemed necessary for competent voting (Scott Althaus's "enlightened preferences" approach)[1] or a simulated public statistically endowed with the knowledge possessed by a PhD in economics (Bryan Caplan's "enlightened public" approach).[2]

According to Brennan, the conclusions that people like Scott Althaus and Bryan Caplan reach based on these surveys form an inference to the best explanation: if people can't answer the survey questions or answer them

1. Althaus 2003.
2. Caplan 2007. Interestingly, Brennan does not question voters' rationality. All in all, he believes, following Bryan Caplan, that voters are rational—or rationally irrational when the incentives warrant it, for example, when they indulge in ideological feel-good beliefs in the context of mass voting where their vote does not matter instrumentally.

differently when they are more knowledgeable, it must be the case that they are not "competent" enough to vote.

Of course, given that democracies are not doing as poorly in the real world as this argument predicts, Brennan must explain away the fact that democracies remain the best existing regime around (by his own admission). His solution is to argue that democracies are not really that democratic to begin with and that their success owes to their elitist or oligarchic elements. Brennan goes one step further. He concludes that if elites are so smart and so effective at compensating for the abysmal stupidity of those who elect them, then maybe we should make our institutions more elitist, for example by restricting the franchise if not altogether replacing elections with test-taking.

When examined closely, however, the empirical evidence supporting Brennan's case for epistemocracy is not conclusive. First, note that this empirical evidence only concerns the ability of citizens to vote and says nothing of their ability to deliberate when put in the proper context. In a deliberative context, data recently compiled by an OECD (Organisation for Economic Co-Operation and Development) report (OECD 2020) shows that over the 289 cases of observed deliberative experiments based on random selection of the participants—thus involving a quasi-average citizen[3]—people are able to engage in thoughtful deliberation about difficult and complex topics and even to make sophisticated policy proposals. In 2004 160 randomly selected Canadians in British

---

3. I say "quasi" because there is a self-selection bias in the sample due to the non-mandatory nature of participation in such experiments.

Columbia came up with a sophisticated electoral reform law proposal (Warren and Pearse 2008). In 2010, in Iceland, a group of 950 randomly selected citizens set the agenda for a group of 25 non-professional politicians to write a new constitution for the country, with the help of the larger public, to which the drafts were regularly crowdsourced online (Landemore 2015). The resulting constitutional proposal holds up well in a comparison with expert drafts written at around the same time, even proving marginally superior to them along some dimensions (Landemore 2017). Most recently, one of the most ambitious deliberative experiment to date, the French Citizens' Convention for Climate, formulated 149 policy proposals on how to reduce French greenhouse gas emissions by 40% of their 1990s levels by 2030 in ways that would be deemed socially fair. The 150 randomly selected citizens were capable of educating themselves on the subject to the point that they, with the help and support of experts and a legal team, could generate ready-to-be-applied law-like proposals, thus meeting the challenge set for them by President Macron.[4]

In light of this counter-evidence, Brennan could also at least entertain the thought that voters' level of information is largely endogenous to the institutions they

4. Most of the analysis is still ongoing and unpublished (in English at least) but for a beginning see Landemore 2020 (Chapters 4 and 5 in particular) and for a variety of perspectives see the Yale-Res Publica online conference "Toward Citizen-Legislators? The Case of the French Citizens' Convention for Climate" held on May 19–21, 2021: https://campuspress.yale.edu/citizenlegislators/.

operate within (see also Maskivker 2019, 118). In our Schumpeterian "democracies," built to minimize voters' participation and leave powers safely in the hand of elected elites, one should not expect in voters more than the minimum amount of information needed to discharge the function of voting every four years. Low levels of information are neither surprising nor decisive about the value of democracy as a regime form, especially since, again, we know that in more demanding contexts citizens are perfectly capable of measuring up to the task. I'll make more of these points in the last section of this essay where I develop a conception of democracy that builds on citizens' expertise, rather than assumes their ignorance and apathy.

However, even if, following Brennan, we take the institutions for granted and strictly focus on the competence of citizens as mere voters within that system, the empirical evidence adduced by Brennan still tells us only so much. Brennan wants us to believe that voters are not even capable of fulfilling the minimal task of voting correctly (i.e., in a minimally informed manner in his view) on predefined options. Whether these options are a choice between party candidate, policy platforms, or referenda questions is irrelevant. But Brennan never seriously addresses the empirical literature on heuristics (e.g., Lupia and McCubbins 1998; Popkin 1994) that show how even voters with little information can use cognitive shortcuts to pass enlightened judgments on a range of issues, including the question of who is competent to make the decisions on their behalf (a.k.a., choosing a competent representative). This elision of confounding empirical evidence is all the more surprising as Brennan later concedes that voters and participants in randomly selected mini-publics must be able to identify expertise even though they can't quite possess it themselves.

Additionally, as I have argued elsewhere (Landemore 2012 and 2014), the metrics and criteria used by political scientists and economists to measure, and then dismiss, the competence of voters are problematically elitist in all kinds of ways (see also Lupia 2006). The literature on voter ignorance generally assumes that certain decontextualized facts or certain experts' beliefs are the appropriate benchmarks for the kind of political knowledge that is needed to make competent political decisions. Yet it's not clear anyone needs to know much about the social sciences, European constitutional treatises, or trade deficits in order to make a judgment about whether globalization or the construction of the European Union benefitted them, their families, and generally the country, and whether a candidate supporting such policies deserves their vote. At any rate this assumption that "information" as measured by political quizzes correlates with the ability to vote "correctly" about common good issues is an assumption, not a fact, and unproven to this day.

Finally, even if we assumed that there was an overwhelming consensus about voter ignorance and bias (and irrationality, though Brennan himself does not question that), I propose that it would still be irrelevant to the discussion about the overall "competence" of voters *and* the instrumental merits of democracy as a regime form. This argument will, I believe, allow me to dispose of the claims that build on the behavioral literature to support an "inference to the best explanation" (if voters do not know certain things then they cannot be competent enough to vote and democracy is doomed to fail).

There is only so much one can conclude from focusing on the properties of the average voter. Democracy is better seen as a system in which voters can avail themselves of group deliberation and majority rule, whether used directly or through representatives, to reach decisions. Collective intelligence, I argued in a book (Landemore 2013), is an emerging property of groups and so it cannot necessarily be observed at the level of individuals or average voters. Furthermore, if it is the case, as I conjecture, that the problem-solving ability of a group is more often a function of the number of members (as a proxy for cognitive diversity and up to a point) than of the average competence of its members, then we will not know enough about the group's potential for smart decision-making if we focus only on the competence of its average member. Approaching the problem from a different angle than my own, Scott Ashworth and Ethan Bueno de Mesquita similarly conclude that the behavioral literature on voter ignorance traffics in illicit inferences about the relationship between individual *inputs* and collective *outcomes*. As they write, "Decontextualized facts about voter characteristics simply do not have any normative implications for democracy one way or the other" (2014, 578). There are too many ways in which deliberation, cognitive diversity, and other factors mediate between individual inputs and collective outcomes.

Systematic biases—such as racism—among the citizenry are of course a very real possibility and any democracy—any regime or collective decision rule, really—needs protections against them. Nothing guarantees than small groups of epistocrats, who may come from the same schools and be very homogenous socially and, often as a result cognitively, are more immune to biases than large groups of diverse people. Additionally, systematic biases would be an issue for my general argument for democracy only if citizens were systematically biased in a correlated way across all possible issues, and if there were no possibility for citizens and their democratic representatives to correct their biases over time. For each case of systematic bias that one could point to, there are many, many more issues where the public is likely to be symmetrically (or randomly) distributed around the right answer if only by being exposed to a variety of points of view, at least in a free society with a sufficiently diverse media.

In an election for political office, for instance, correlated biases on one issue may not matter because the candidate will be assessed across many issues.[5] To adapt a passage of my book *Democratic Reason*, "Assuming minimally sophisticated voters relative to the questions at hand and a liberal-democratic society, or at least a pre-voting context, encouraging dissent and diverse thinking, . . . Caplan's [and I assume Brennan's] worst case scenario of a situation

---

5. It is true that in referenda, for example, which I am not defending here specifically, a systematic bias on one issue will matter since issues are decided one by one. For such cases, I would argue, the answer is not less democracy, but more public deliberation. We may be tempted by the short-cut to experts (e.g., economists, Supreme Court justices) in some instances—and that might well be a good idea under time constraints or given the practical necessities of a division of epistemic labor. But, again, purely epistemically speaking, I think we are safer with the inclusiveness of the deliberative democratic process.

in which the average error is high and diversity low [across the board of all political issues]—the condition for the worst case scenario of systematically abysmally unintelligent democracies—is not very plausible" (Landemore 2013, 197). By contrast, small oligarchies of "knowers" may be more prone to the dangers of group think, especially if they don't have to be accountable to a large, critical, and diverse society. The "best and brightest" as we know from history can produce abysmally stupid decisions. The question is always comparative: of the many ordinary citizens and the supposedly best and most virtuous, who does it less often? On my view, which focuses less on individuals' contributions and more on the systemic properties of the group (cognitive diversity as approximated by numbers), democracy is what turns the "lead of individual contributions" into the gold of democratic reason, making it superior to competing, less inclusive regimes.

OBJECTION TWO: WHAT IS THE RELEVANCE OF A DEDUCTIVE ARGUMENT TO REAL-LIFE DEMOCRACIES?

Jason Brennan (2014) has pointed out that my epistemic defense of democracy is a priori or deductive, based on formal results, including my own "Numbers Trump Ability" Theorem, not empirical evidence. He suggests that democracy's epistemic superiority cannot be conclusively established that way. By contrast, he offers a critique of democracy that he claims is empirical, based on the documented ignorance and systematic biases of voters in some existing countries. Brennan's critique, on the face of it, depends on both a methodological and epistemological commitment to the inductive method in the social sciences as the only way to "prove" anything, and on the claim that my demonstration is just irrelevant theory. I want to challenge both positions.

My view about the proper role of the deductive and inductive methods in the social sciences is pluralist and pragmatic. To the extent that our concern is to explain phenomena in the social world (whether one can conclusively "prove" the validity of any explanation seems to be a taller order), I think it will require a mix of methods, partly depending on the object at stake. I would argue that both the deductive and inductive methods are useful and relevant to the making of causal claims about social phenomena.[6]

Brennan might still want to ask: What is the point of a deductive proof? How will showing that an idealized version of democracy—a model—"works," in the sense of doing better than a model oligarchy under idealized conditions, help us understand whether real democracies in the real world work? Moreover, is it not real democracies that really concerns us? Space does not permit a lengthy defense of model thinking.[7] I will however emphasize that the use of models (e.g., simplified or abstract representations) of

6. See Elster and Landemore 2018 for my general philosophy of the social sciences.
7. See instead the excellent work by Michael Weisberg (2013) on this. Scott E. Page (2018) also has some very interesting thoughts on this; for an intriguing take on the role of models in political theory, see Johnson 2014.

real objects is helpful in explaining the world we live in. In particular, models help us construct plausible stories regarding the mechanisms behind familiar, observable phenomena, such as the flying of planes, the functioning of the market, the logic of collective action, or, in this case, the processes of problem-solving and knowledge aggregation in real democracies. In other words, for empirical realities, my deductive approach is "hypothesis-generating" (see Landemore 2014 for a longer exploration of the philosophy of science behind my views and Johnson forthcoming for a defense of model thinking).

The irony, as it turns out, is that Brennan's argument is just as deductive as mine when it comes to generating the crucial conclusion that democracies are dysfunctional regimes. Indeed, the empirical literature on which Brennan relies does not empirically "prove" that democracy is not smart. It only proves, at best, that individual citizens are not. Brennan's argument in support of the claim that the collective aggregation of citizens' input does not produce good results is purely deductive too! Empirical evidence about voter ignorance is (implicitly) plugged into a rational choice model of the mechanism connecting voters' preferences to collective outcomes (the median voter theorem, more or less). The model spits out the conclusion that democracy cannot possibly be smart. Democracy must be garbage out because it is garbage in.

Brennan's posturing as an empiricist (incidentally using other people's data rather than generating his own, whereas I can at least claim to have conducted some empirical work to test my hypotheses) is somewhat puzzling. As far as I can tell, Downs's theory of rational ignorance and Caplan's very similar theory of rational irrationality, which

Brennan uses to generate his negative conclusions about democracy, are entirely deductive. They are, essentially, rational choice theoretical results. There is thus a certain chutzpah in denying advocates of democracy such as myself the resources of a priori or (more accurately) deductive thinking when Brennan helps himself to those very same tools.

The reality is that Brennan does not provide empirical evidence that democracies are garbage out since his empirical focus is the input.[8] Ultimately, the most that Brennan demonstrates is that the American system sometimes chooses suboptimal policies and could perform better on some issues than it currently does. I do not dispute that much more limited and plausible point.

I will, however, point to empirical literature that suggests that democracies perform well in many domains.

First, there is micro-evidence supporting the benefits of democratic decision-making at the scale of very small groups. Lab experiments in psychology show that mini-democracies outperform mini-oligarchies in terms of decision-making (e.g., Curşeu et al. 2013). Field

---

8. More problematically, some of Brennan's seemingly empirical claims, like the mapping of voters into apathetic and ignorant Hobbits, ideological and partisan Hooligans, and scientific and rational appear largely made up. As Julia Maskivker points out, the way Brennan partitions the world, without much empirical support, plausibly ignores a fourth class of voters—she calls them MIV (moderately interested voters)—who are people who won't do well on a political scientists' test between elections but who do their "due diligence" around election time (Maskivker 2019, 83) and whose sufficiently informed views might well be shaping majoritarian views.

experiments show that villages that make decisions democratically outperform villages making decisions in less participatory ways (e.g., Goree and Leeat 2011; Olken 2010; Wantchekon 2012). I have gathered some empirical evidence on the matter by comparing the constitutional proposals put forward by experts to those suggested by ordinary citizens in the context of the Icelandic quasi-natural experiment of the 2010–2011 constitutional process (Landemore 2017). I showed in this research that the inclusiveness of the process—achieved through a national forum of 950 randomly selected people before the drafting stage and the diversity of citizen expertise present on the council in charge of writing the draft, as well as the crowdsourcing of the draft during the writing process—contributed to the production of a marginally but crucially better, richer, more liberal and democratic text overall.

At the macro scale of countries, existing empirical studies support the claim that democracies perform well by many standards, such as avoiding war with other democracies, dealing with famines, and aggregating factual knowledge efficiently (e.g., Spencer 1998; Sen 1999; Lindert 2003; Ober 2008). An ambitious observational study in economics (Acemoglu et al. 2018) claims to show that democracy "promotes economic growth"[9] and "increases future GDP by encouraging investment, increasing schooling, inducing

9. A questionable goal in the age of planetary resources exhaustion but still one valued by governments the world over.

economic reforms, improving public good provision, and reducing social unrest."[10]

I do not want to make too much of this macro-evidence for my argument because such claims are always disputed. Besides, existing regimes are not pure democracies and contain too many moving parts, including parts that are not democratic per se (the rule of law, a constitutional system, liberal rights, free markets, etc.,), such that it is hard to attribute global epistemic outcomes to specifically democratic features (such as inclusive deliberation and majority rule with universal suffrage). Similarly, Classical Athens was as much a patriarchy of slave-owners as a democracy with respect to its citizens. For "mini-democracies" tested in laboratory experiments and Deliberative Polls, I think the explanatory stories I point to (the "Numbers Trump Ability Theorem" for deliberation; Condorcet's Jury Theorem and the Miracle of Aggregation or the Diversity Theorem for aggregation) are extremely plausible. For actual mass representative democracies, however, there may well be too many moving parts to conclude anything.

But, conversely, since we still know so little about why actual democracies "work" in the real world, I do not

10. Most strikingly, the authors claim to quantify the impact of democracy on GDP: "Our central estimates suggest that a country that switches from nondemocracy to democracy achieves about 20 percent higher GDP per capita in the long run (or roughly in the next 30 years). Our results indicate no differential effect of democracy on economic growth by the initial level of economic development, though there is some evidence that democracy is more conducive to higher GDP in countries that start out with higher levels of education."

see why the skeptics and the critics of democracy should have the upper hand. At best, we can conclude that Jason Brennan and I are at a stalemate and that more research is needed. My conjecture is that democracies' epistemic merits exist in large part due to the inclusive and egalitarian properties of their central deliberative institutions. Moving in the direction of less democracy would worsen rather than improve their performance.

Brennan's next move, in his book as well as the above essay, is to claim that epistocracy would do even better than democracy. I now turn from a defense of democracy to a critique of epistocracy.

Chapter 7

Against Epistocracies

IN THIS CHAPTER, I BUTTRESS THE positive case for democracy presented so far with a negative argument against various kinds of epistocracies, including Chinese-style pure meritocracy, technocracy on the model of the European Union, and majoritarian epistocracy in the vein that Brennan advocates. Note that in these arguments, I will not make what is perhaps the most straightforward argument against epistocracies (especially oligarchic ones): the argument from corruption. I assume throughout that corruption is not more prevalent among epistocracies than among democracies, or that it could be curbed in some institutionally robust way.

AGAINST PURE MERITOCRACY

Consider first the argument in favor of meritocracy developed by Daniel Bell in his book *The China Model*. China notoriously managed to lift six hundred million people out of poverty over the last forty years. Bell surmises that what the regime is doing well is putting people with the right kind of knowledge and moral ethos in charge. Bell is convinced that China is a meritocracy and

Debating Democracy. Jason Brennan and Hélène Landemore, Oxford University Press. © Oxford University Press 2022. DOI: 10.1093/oso/9780197540817.003.0009

it does not really matter for the argument here that this description is contested, including by Chinese scholars (e.g., Cheng 2011). Bell also argues that Chinese meritocracy, at least as he reconstructs it, is the only regime capable of handling the size and complexity of politics at the continental scale. Bell, finally, assumes that China's epistemocracy is as virtuous as it is wise. (Brennan, by contrast, has no such illusions about epistocrats in power, and counts on classic checks-and-balances mechanisms to ensure that the knowers rule for the public good rather than for themselves.)

Bell's argument, I should acknowledge, is not so much a universal theoretical claim about meritocracy's superiority over democracy as a plea for cultural and political contextualism. What is good for the US (more dubiously so, as recent history suggests) might not be good for China. Furthermore, Bell highlights the risks of destabilization involved in calling for the democratization of a regime that does not have the required cultural heritage (though it is dubious that there is any actual consensus about this heritage in China). Considering the disastrous results of attempts to export democracy to the Middle East and elsewhere, the point is not without merit. The book is, overall, an effort to take seriously a political model often uncritically reviled in the West, and surely Bell deserves credit for nudging Western political theorists out of their complacency.

Nevertheless, I will examine Bell's contextual arguments at a higher level of generality, in order to see if a more abstract case for the superiority of epistocracy over democracy can stand.

Bell advances six arguments for Chinese meritocracy, including

1. the stability of the regime,
2. the sociological legitimacy it has accrued over many decades,
3. its compatibility with basic human rights and a range of democratic values,
4. the claim that a meritocracy is better suited to long-term and universal responsibilities,
5. the complexity-due-to-size argument, and
6. the argument from speed and efficiency.

Rather than consider all these arguments, which may or may not all have merits, let me focus on the one with the clearest epistemic dimension, the argument from complexity due to size, which neatly translates into other contexts as well. Indeed, the very same argument is often used in the case of the European Union to defend what critics see as its technocratic aspects and its "democratic deficit."

Meritocracy, for Bell, is a regime in which both agenda-setting and final decision-making, are in the hands of a relatively small number of people (compared to the rest of the population). These people have the epistemic credentials of "political knowers," credentials measured by exam-based evaluations, past political experience, and tested moral virtue.[1] Technically, epistocracy or rule of the knowers does not have to mean minority rule (and indeed it does not

---

1. Technically, I'm not sure that moral virtue is a requirement for epistocrats, since external mechanisms could take care of giving them the right incentives, but this is not relevant to our analysis.

in Brennan's version, as we shall see below). But, in practice, the excellence presupposed by meritocracy does mean restricting access to power to a minority because excellence is, by definition, rare. In general, it is fair to assume that by epistocracy we mean rule by the most knowledgeable, (not just, as Brennan does, the sufficiently knowledgeable).

Note that political meritocracy thus defined is an alternative to democracy, not a bureaucracy meant to support any regime form. Daniel Bell often stresses that political meritocracy rules out a one-person-one-vote system as well as multi-party, or even two-party elections to select top leaders. Indeed, there is but one party in China, the Chinese Communist Party (CCP), the governing structure of which is strictly hierarchical and topped by a Politburo of 25 members, itself crowned by a central committee of so-called "magnificent seven." Below the highest decision-making levels, there is a Central Committee of about 205 members, which heads a Party Congress of around 2,200 members. At best, therefore, the meritocrats in China form an infinitesimal minority in this country of 1.4 billion people. What is even more striking than the rejection of elections and a multi-party system is the fact that agenda-setting and the final say about questions of public interest are in the hands of a tiny minority. This minority is almost exclusively male (the magnificent seven have never included women and the top 25 have only included at most 2) and of Han ethnicity. No matter how consultative the regime claims to be, decision-making remains, ultimately, in the hands of a few homogenous people.

Let me now turn to the "complexity-due-to size argument," which can be reduced to the more general "complexity" argument. This is arguably one of the most

powerful points to be made in defense of epistemocracy/
meritocracy. This argument challenges the view that ordinary citizens, or their elected leaders or otherwise selected
representatives, can deal with the complex problems that
a continental-scale country, or perhaps any country in an
increasingly complex world, faces. However, complexity
is not the main problem that polities face, nor is it fundamentally new. Complexity is a secondary problem that
arises after we have a better sense of the problems we
face. Uncertainty and complexity are often conflated, in
part because uncertainty can be the result of complexity, but they are not the same. Political uncertainty is
the epistemic situation we face when we lack knowledge
about the kinds of problems—the bundle of issues if you
will—that the polity will have to negotiate. Complexity,
by contrast, is about the multiplicity of dimensions that
a political problem, once we know what it is, may present
and the amount of knowledge it may require to be solved.[2]
Complexity arises as soon as we leave the setting of a small
insulated community (a tribe in the Amazonian forest
perhaps). Uncertainty, however, is always there, consub-
stantial with the human existence in the face of a largely
unpredictable future. Uncertainty, however, is probably
low in a small, insulated community and maximal in the
current globalized world of highly interactive political entities. High uncertainty in turn increases the complexity of

2. In fact there is an irreducible amount of uncertainty even
   once we know what the problems are about the exact nature
   of the facts involved but for the sake of argument, I'll leave
   that present uncertainty out of the equation here, stacking
   the deck against my own claims.

decision-making in the world. Fundamentally, the problem of politics is thus uncertainty about the bundle of problems the world (including the world of our community, with its complex social logics) throws at us.

Epistocracies are poorly suited to handle political uncertainty because they unduly restrict the set of decision-makers and the resulting cognitive diversity of the decision-making group. Once the problems are identified, do epistocracies have an advantage over democracies? I don't see why they necessarily should. Citizens or their democratic representatives (whether elected or, as I would prefer, randomly selected) can rely on and avail themselves of the expertise of bureaucrats and experts too, while funneling it through a much more diverse set of cognitive perspectives and lived experiences. Elected legislatures in current democracies are thus constantly calling on expert commissions and testimonies while still retaining the prerogative of authoring the laws (and so could members of a randomly selected legislature in an open democracy model, more on which in my last chapter). Of course epistocrat can augment and expand their own knowledge and perspectives by consulting large amounts of people, including the public (as Chinese authorities regularly do). It could thus be that a democracy backed up by experts and bureaucrats on the one hand and a highly consultative epistocracy on the other would draw a stalemate. I would hypothesize, however, (though I do not have evidence for it), that cognitive diversity at the point of decision-making, rather than upstream of it, is what really matters, thus favoring, howsoever slightly, an expert-informed democracy over a consultative epistocracy.

Now, were the domain of political decision-making narrow and precisely defined, then one could at least plausibly claim that a subgroup of experts is likely to outperform democratic rulers.[3] For example, if the goal were economic growth and economic growth only, then maybe rule by economists would be best. However, politics is not such a technical, narrowly and precisely defined domain of questions. Politics is a "fuzzy" domain, where *uncertainty* is as much the problem as complexity, and where increasing complexity itself is likely to generate more uncertainty. Economic policies always create all kinds of unpredictable effects, which the public is going to experience in all their diversity. Their input is the decision-making process would thus seem crucial.

Similarly, it might be true that we would probably want to give more weight to, say, an economist's vote in a decision about bank capitalization than to a random person on the street. But this preference for experts applies only once we (as a group) are already in a position to identify the nature of the problems at hand and to determine who is best situated to answer them. At that point, we are no longer trying to predict whose voice and votes will matter more in the resolution of future problems, because the problems have gone from possibility to reality. We can thus proceed to make decisions about these particular problems through the various means at our disposal, including experts. In other words, delegating to experts or a subset of people who have plausible credentials for the task at hand can only be done as a secondary step, not a first one,

3.

once we have moved from a situation of uncertainty to one of risk.

One question one might ask at this point: let's admit that the superiority of democracies over epistocracies is in being able to come up through inclusive collective deliberation with better plans to solve collective problems. In the end though, even a democracy needs to delegate the implementation of the plan to agencies and experts. If so, isn't there a risk of epistocratic rule coming back through the back door, via the power of these agencies and experts to whom so much implementation power is delegated? Let's say a democracy creates an OSHA (Occupational Safety and Health Administration) and authorizes it to issue workplace safety rules; or it creates an EPA (Environmental Protection Agency) and authorizes it to regulate activities producing environmental pollution and affecting climate change. Isn't that rule by experts in the end?

Not necessarily. First, it is not a trivial difference between democracies and epistocracies that citizens or their democratic representatives have the first say over experts in the former and not in the latter. Path-dependency is crucial and who gets to set the agenda makes a huge difference. Second, even at the stage where much of the decision-making process and implementation is delegated to experts and administrative agencies, there should be a way for citizens to keep "experts on tap, not on top." This phrase, sometimes credited to Winston Churchill but in fact first coined by the editor of an Irish paper, George William Russel, in 1910,[4] has now achieved

---

4. For the genealogy of that quote, see https://quoteinvestigator.com/2019/01/26/expert/.

the status of folk theorem in democratic participatory circles. It neatly summarizes the spirit in which experts, as well as administrators and bureaucrats, should be mobilized in an authentic democracy. Keeping experts on tap and preventing them from getting on top can be facilitated by classic accountability mechanisms, from carefully cultivated professional norms and guidelines to institutions such as ethics committees. Better still, it can be achieved by ensuring the presence of citizens within expert and administrative circles, as supervisors or as co-constructors of the decision-making process. At a minimum citizens can be present to accompany and inform the work of agencies, administrations, and experts. A recent example of such an attempt at embedding citizens' wisdom into an expert process is the citizen jury of thirty-five randomly selected citizens that was tasked with accompanying the 2021 governmental vaccination campaign in France.

It is true, of course, that a democracy with a large administrative and bureaucratic apparatus could turn into an epistocracy of sorts, where all the power ends up in the hands of experts. But the point is, it need not to. The key is in the overall design: who has the first say, who has the last say, and who is present in the room where key deliberations take place and decisions get made? Is there transparency throughout? Are there accountability mechanisms such that the experts will be constantly reminded that they are here to serve, not dominate? Finally, are there participatory designs that allow citizens to be part of the expert processes?

Notice that, even in a context of complexity but no real uncertainty (a context of risk), solving problems democratically may still present advantages. The trade-off between more or less inclusive as well as more or less egalitarian decision rules will then depend on various concerns, including the cost of mistakes associated with each decision rule. If, for example, democracy reliably avoids the most egregious mistakes, it might be the superior decision rule in the context of risk even if it leads to a slightly higher *number* of (less costly) mistakes being made.[5] Switching from considering all the included individuals as epistemic peers to weighing them unequally may perhaps be justified, but only once we have moved from a situation where we are trying to figure out the nature of the problem coming at us to a situation where the problem is clearly identified and the needed expertise more obvious. In the first situation, if it turns out that the next bubble to burst is related to, say, students' debt, it might be important to have retained some college freshmen or recent graduates whose payments are coming due in the decision pool.

Part of my reasoning throughout owes to the argument by psychologist Gerd Gigerenzer (2014) about the relative performance of simple rules of thumb versus complex models in any domain of life characterized by a degree of uncertainty. Let me introduce this argument here.

Based on years of empirical studies, Gigerenzer generalizes that three conditions must hold for a simple heuristic

---

5. As per the distinction between probability and expectation, it does not matter how often a procedure (or investment strategy) is wrong; what matters is the average expected value of that decision-rule (Taleb 2005, 99).

(or "rule of thumb") to be preferable to a complex equation or model:

1. The predictive uncertainty is large.
2. The number of N is large. In Gigerenzer's model, that number refers to the range of options between which one must decide.
3. The learning sample (i.e., the available past data) is small

Applying his reasoning to stock market investment, where all three conditions apply, Gigerenzer argues that an investor is better off diversifying her portfolio following the simple heuristic "One over N"—i.e., divide your money equally over all available stocks—rather than following a mean-variance strategy, which is a complex calculation aiming to optimize the expected return of a stock against a given level of risk.

Now let us apply the reasoning to the rival heuristics "democracy" and "oligarchy." The beauty of the first one is its simplicity: divide power equally among all (both voices and votes) regardless of competence and differences between individuals. The heuristic "oligarchy" or even "plural voting," however, is more complex to implement, as one first needs to figure out criteria by which to exclude or include people, sometimes in proportion to their measured incompetence. But recall that the simple heuristic is only preferrable under the three conditions described above. So we have to ask ourselves, first: How large is uncertainty in politics? I already argued that a large degree of uncertainty in politics is a rather un-heroic assumption to make.

Second, how large is the relevant N in politics? Here we are considering the numbers of possible decision-makers (one, few, or many), rather than the range of options to decide on. In mass industrialized democracies, N—the number of potential decision-makers—is very large indeed. It is even quite large if we restrict our focus to the representatives of the people, who usually number somewhere in the hundreds in existing parliaments. Finally, how big is the learning sample in politics? That is, how many years of data about the judgment of past decision-makers do we have to feed complicated oligarchic models aiming to allocate a greater number of votes to the more competent people? Democrats and advocates of epistocracies seem to have a different answer to that question. Daniel Bell argues that in the case of China there is ample evidence for the past judgment of Chinese rulers because they climb the party ladder by proving their competence at generating economic growth at the local level first. It is thus possible, for him, to assign more weight to the people who have proven the superiority of their political judgment over time.

I, on the other hand, find it doubtful that this data has much value as a basis for prediction. Past competence at the local level (assuming it can be accurately measured) may not translate straightforwardly into competence at the national level. Additionally, adding up individual competences may not result in the smartest group, if these people end up thinking too similarly (see previous chapters). In any case, even if we could accumulate enough data about past "knowers" among us (as people who got a number of things right in the past), this would presumably be for domain-specific issues such as foreign policy or economics, not for the universal category of politics. So, to the extent that Bell's argument works at all, it only works if politics is always about the same single issue, such as economic growth. But if the goal is to staff a generalist Congress as opposed to a multitude of issue-specific assemblies, I don't see how we will ever be able to identify universal knowers because no one can have the amount and diversity of knowledge required to address all possible political issues. The failure of traditional Confucian meritocracy is a case in point. The imperial exam system that prioritized the acquisition of certain types of knowledge led to the social under-appreciation of other, more technical, types of knowledge and eventually suppressed intellectual innovation in Imperial China, which in turn rendered the country unprepared for the great power competition of the nineteenth century (see also Mokyr 2016).[6]

And even if we managed to accumulate extensive knowledge on a wide range of issues, perhaps all issues, the causal structure of the world may well change faster than we can accumulate the relevant data, such that the data will always only help predict the world of yesterday as opposed to the world of tomorrow. The promise of big data in politics, which would allow us to identify a decision rule giving more weight to the more knowledgeable than the simple heuristic "political equality," is thus bound to remain unfulfilled.[7]

6. I thank Zhichao Tong for this last point and for the example of the failure of Confucian meritocracy.
7. I leave out for now the more difficult question of a generalist artificial intelligence capable of generating better governance than any form of human rule, whether democratic or epistocratic.

If this is true, then all of Gigerenzer's conditions apply and the simple heuristics "democracy" is better adapted to the political ecology of politics than any more complicated scheme involving an uneven distribution of power.

Bell senses the problem at various places in his book. He recognizes that as China's potential for economic growth diminishes, "The more serious threat to the Chinese political system is that economic growth will lose its status as the main source of legitimacy" (Bell 2015: xxi). Today China's problems are more diverse—he mentions "rampant pollution, a huge gap between rich and poor, precarious social welfare, and an explosion of government debt, not to mention massive corruption" (Bell 2015: xxi). However, on what criteria should we choose leaders when matters become so diverse and increasingly unpredictable?

Bell has no choice but to acknowledge that, when the domain of politics becomes open-ended and fuzzy, as opposed to being narrowly restricted to goals like "economic growth,"

> things become more complicated for a political system that prides itself on meritocratic mechanisms for the selection and promotion of leaders. Should government officials be assessed according to their ability to deliver economic growth, to improve social welfare, to reduce corruption, to protect the environment, to reduce the gap between rich and poor, to reduce government debt, or to achieve some combination of these goals? (Bell 2015: xxi–xxii).

Bell interestingly concludes that the only solution for the Chinese government is to obtain "more input from the people, not just to help decide on priorities, but also to take the heat off when large constituencies are unhappy with some policies" (Bell 2015: xxii). This kind of popular consultation is an echo of the "mass line," a political, organizational, and leadership method invented by Mao Zedong that consisted of consulting the masses, interpreting their suggestions within the framework of Marxism-Leninism, and then enforcing the resulting policies. The reasoning for it in Bell is, strikingly, both instrumental, indeed downright epistemic, and intrinsic: "Such openness is necessary not just *to improve decision making* but also *to diffuse the sense of responsibility for those decisions*" (Bell 2015: xxii). In other words, opening up the decision-process to the people will improve decisions and make a larger number of people experience a sense (perhaps an illusion) of agency or at least responsibility for the decision.

Bell thus wants to have his cake and eat it too. He wants meritocracies to have the advantages of the collective intelligence of the people without having to surrender actual power to them. Indeed, even to the extent that these consultation processes are causally influential on policy (which would be something), the expertocrats maintain final control all the way through. Openness for Bell thus means mere consultation, not actual access to power (as in the model of "open democracy" I defend myself in the next chapter).

Bell further assumes that it is enough for such consultation, deliberation, and participation to take place "at lower levels of government." He extrapolates that whatever information is garnered there will percolate up the political hierarchy, or else that the benefits of consultation at higher levels are not worth the costs. It is only at lower levels of government that Bell is willing to promote electoral democracy and even to experiment with the "innovations of modern democratic societies, such as open public hearings, deliberative polling, and referenda on key issues" (Bell 2015: xxii)

Can mere consultation inject as much cognitive diversity into the system as choosing representatives based on one person, one vote, or an even more democratic selection mechanism like a lottery? As already hinted above, I am skeptical that merely listening to people and integrating their input to a decision, will yield the same results as empowering them to set the agenda and make decisions themselves. For one thing, people will not be as invested and honest in giving their input if they are not sure that what they say matters. Worse, they may suspect that the government may instrumentalize this input as participatory window-dressing for decisions that have already been made. This is a major problem with purely consultative processes. Second, even if the input from the people ends up being highly informative, the problem remains that it will pass and be filtered throgh the cognitive processes of a small, elite group of people with similar ways of thinking, mitigating the initial gains from wide consultation.

The main epistemic problem facing regimes like the Chinese meritocracy or the European Union technocracy is thus vulnerability to cognitive blind spots that carry potentially devastating consequences. Further, because the pool of decision-makers is not refreshed frequently, epistocracies are likely to reinforce biases born from those blind spots, and thus become worse over time.

In conclusion, let me introduce two new arguments against epistocracies that I borrow from the exciting work of a new generation of epistemic democrats. A first argument is that technocracies are more prone to irrationality than democracies because the former's incentive structures render them insulated from the public they are meant to serve. Matthew Coleman (2019) thus argues that even if the information was made available otherwise and even with the best intentions, without popular accountability, technocrats would still be likely to choose suboptimal policies. He borrows examples from the European Union which, in recent years, has imposed austerity policies on Southern states like Greece that not only were rejected by national governments but objectively inflicted enormous social and economic harm in the short and medium term with dubious long-term economic effects. When faced with the unpopularity and bad outcomes of their policies, however, Euro technocrats doubled down on bad policy, "reaffirming the technocratic basis of their authority by sticking to 'rules' derived from supranational institutions even as they failed to right the Eurozone's economic ship" (Mathijs and Blyth 2018, cited in Coleman 2019). Austerity policies, though globally irrational (bad for the polity) were indeed locally rational (good for the careers of these technocrats). Put differently, the policies were perhaps politically rational, gaining experts the approval of their superiors and helping them progress in the bureaucratic hierarchy, but economically suboptimal (i.e., not serving the common good) (Coleman 2019 citing Mathijs and Blyth 2018, 112–113). For Coleman, it is insulation from democratic feedback that "allowed [European technocrats] to learn the wrong lessons as the crisis went on—a skewed process of social learning that could have been improved if the preferences of the electorate had been included in decision-making" (Coleman 2019).

The second argument comes from Zhichao Tong, an "epistemic realist," who defends democracy on the grounds of its epistemic competitiveness under what he calls "the circumstances of international politics" (Tong 2020), namely the uncertainty that comes from the competition between states on the international stage (This uncertainty is but a subset of the general political uncertainty I talked about earlier). Tong also uses Miranda Fricker's epistemic injustice framework to point out some additional limits of epistocracies. Over the long term, Tong argues, political meritocracy is likely to amplify the epistemic arrogance of political elites. Being defined as "the smartest and the brightest" means that these elites will systematically overestimate the accuracy of their judgment and conversely underestimate that of the rest of the population. Many elected officials in Western democracies share this prejudice when their electability is in part due to their meritocratic education (think Oxbridge club in England or the graduates from Grandes Écoles and l'ENA in France). This arrogance, in turn, renders governmental officials *epistemically unreceptive* to the opinions of ordinary citizens, which is why even well-intentioned consultation cannot work in a political meritocracy, "because meritocracy as an ideology leads to further increases of credibility excesses and credibility deficits (to use Miranda Fricker's framework) in the society that makes any kind of meaningful communication between mass and elite difficult." As Tong further states, it is important to acknowledge this point because "only a particular kind of the rule of the few, namely meritocracy or epistocracy, has this problem." Oligarchies based on wealth could acknowledge that their power is not based on intellectual superiority or greater knowledge and thus suffer less from epistemic arrogance.[8]

This is not to say, however, that a commitment to the principle of mass consultation or the mass line ideology is not an epistemic improvement on the whole, including for epistocracies. As Tong puts it, "Had CCP followed Bell's suggestion and completely abandoned socialism by changing its name to "the Chinese Meritocratic Union" (see page 197 of Bell's *The China Model*), it would probably have become an epistemically more arrogant, and hence less efficient, organization. In this regard, the epistemic success of contemporary China is due to its divergence from, rather than convergence with, Bell's pure meritocratic ideal."[9]

AGAINST MAJORITARIAN EPISTOCRACIES

Hitherto, I have argued against classic epistocracy as embodied, in particular, by the Chinese meritocracy and the European Union technocracy. Jason Brennan, however, has called for a more democratic version of epistocracy, characterized by what he sees as a small dent in the universal franchise. Brennan advocates not for minority

8. Zhichao Tong, personal communication on July 29, 2020. See also Zhichao 2020a and 2020b.
9. See note 28 supra.

rule per se but rather for a system in which the most ignorant or unsophisticated 5% of citizens are excluded from voting. Brennan says that he does not necessarily reject the principles of equality and inclusion but suggests that, on the grounds of efficiency and for epistemic reasons, we need to restrict input on policy-making to people with the right epistemic credentials. He objects to the principle of "one person, one vote" at the margin, rather than at a fundamental level.

And indeed, if some people systematically underperform on political literacy quizzes designed by smart political scientists who know the kind of relevant social scientific knowledge one would want in a citizen, why don't we decrease the voice of these underperformers or silence them altogether to save them from "polluting the polls" (Brennan 2009) as well as, presumably, public debate? According to Brennan, the fact that this tiny 5% might correspond to otherwise socially, economically, and racially marginalized populations (e.g., uneducated, poor Black women) might be unfortunate. However, this would be an argument for improving social and economic inequalities as well as eradicating structural racism, not for including these epistemically inferior populations in public debate and the voting process (Brennan 2016, 228).

The racially problematic implications of this argument should give us pause and are by themselves enough to disqualify it in practice. However, we can take this argument on its own, purely theoretical and epistemic terms. Brennan's defense of epistocracy is interesting because, typically, the epistocratic alternatives to democracy are forms of minority rule—and indeed rule by tiny groups of people (aristocrats, plutocrats, technocrats . . .). But what Brennan defends is not minority rule. Instead, he defends an exclusionary form of majority rule, where the vast majority—95% of people in his version—are considered knowledgeable enough and thus retain voting rights, and only a small percentage of the population is deprived of a say because they don't know enough. Brennan thus defends a variety of majoritarian epistocracy, the rule of the knowledgeable 95%.

As Brennan sees it, the epistemic argument I have developed allows me to disqualify minority rule but not the rule of the epistemically superior 95%. By my own argument, he claims, I should be fine with the rule of "the many-but-not-quite-everybody" (Brennan 2016, 185). In other words, even though he agrees that it is probably the case that many heads are better than one, he disagrees that my argument takes us to "*all* heads are better than one." What would be lost, he asks, epistemically speaking, if we excluded only a tiny percentage of objectively incompetent people? By objectively incompetent people Brennan does not mean the mentally ill, or people with degenerative neurological diseases like Alzheimer's, since those are a tiny fraction of the population and do not vote for the most part even when they retain the right. The individuals that Brennan means to exclude are the healthy, mentally fit people who simply cannot pass a relatively simple political test devised by social scientists.

My first question to Brennan is this: What would such exclusion achieve? Recall that in my model deliberation does most of the epistemic work. Most filtering of bad input or bad reasoning occurs at that deliberative stage. So there is no reason not to include everyone as one more, howsoever uninformed, voice will not pollute the outcome but will at most delay the conclusion of the deliberation. I suspect that Brennan's focus on the pure aggregation of judgments (votes) rather than on deliberation is what makes him so willing to exclude people. In pure judgment aggregation, there is an exact trade-off between inclusiveness and group competence. Including even a few incompetent voices may diminish the aggregated value of the collective decision.

Brennan thus assumes that there is an epistemic cost to including incompetent people in collective decision-making and that the outcome of collective decision-making would necessarily be improved by preventatively silencing some people. When applied to my model, Brennan's proposal entails silencing the least competent 5% of the population both in terms of their right to participate in deliberation and their voting rights. In practice, this means that the excluded 5% cannot elect representatives (or have a right to enter civic lotteries under my open democracy model, more on which in the next chapter).

In one sense, Brennan is correct. For many questions, perhaps even all possible questions in the short term, outcomes would not necessarily be epistemically worse, or at any rate very different, if we excluded 5% of the population based on the political literacy tests he recommends (assuming that the excluded people would otherwise have been active in politics). After all, Brennan could get lucky! At the very least it is possible that in very specific one-question referendums, such as the UK referendum on Brexit, disenfranchising the least literate 5% (by his own standard) would not have worsened the result and might even have improved it. Not all of us add something to the conversation, or to the pool of votes, at all times. Many of us make mistakes or hold incorrect views throughout our lives.

Recall, however, that my argument is *not* intended to work for just one or a few issues, or just in the short term (where luck plays a huge role), or once we know what issues fate has thrown at us. It is meant to be true in expectation over the long term and across the board of possible issues. Brennan's limited epistocracy is, by contrast, unnecessarily fragile, especially over the long term, in the face of changing circumstances and problems. It could only work if we had a clear sense of what the questions were going to be (preferably the questions that correspond to the political science quizzes he has in mind) or if the world did not change too much or too fast. As time goes by and circumstances change, however, it becomes very likely that his epistocracy will run into issues where it will miss the very voices and votes it purposely excluded. Even if the probability is low, the expected cost might still be huge. Why take the risk?

There may be a short window of time in which a Brennanist epistocracy would work, perhaps even better than a democracy. But probabilistically, this superiority is bound to vanish over time. The question is when. In the famous paradox of the Sorites, the important problem was the boundary between a heap and a non-heap. Here we face the problem of determining the boundary between the predictable future and the unpredictable one, and thus the boundary between the domain in which an inegalitarian decision rule is appropriate and the one in which an egalitarian rule is better. Even if such a boundary exists, it is unknowable. Where should we draw the line between the short term and the long term? At what point do we take away the decision power from the epistocrats and redistribute it more equitably? The idea that there is such a thing as a predictable short-term horizon in which the nature and structure of problems are stable is a result of hindsight bias. Only in retrospect are we able to identify historically "stable" short-term periods, like, say, a business cycle or a long peace. Ex ante, however, it is impossible to tell whether Apple stocks will keep rising or if we are on the eve of another 9/11 or Great Recession or—God forbid—Great War. In politics, as in economics, timing is everything (and getting it wrong can be extremely costly).

Let me return to the point I made early in this essay about political uncertainty: inclusiveness on egalitarian grounds is the most parsimonious way to get us the cognitive diversity we need.

I repeat myself, but it is a difficult point to understand and thus worth insisting on. One can rationally pick and choose the heads one lets into the conversation or count in a vote (e.g., to maximize expert credentials or to maximize cognitive diversity concerning a given problem) *only if we have already identified and defined the problem*. For the tasks that confront a deliberative generalist assembly of democratic representatives, there is no such certainty nor a well-defined set of tasks. That is why my argument for democracy hinges not just on the Diversity Trumps Ability Theorem, as Brennan keeps mistakenly arguing (Brennan 2016, 185 and again his reply to my views in this book) but *on my generalization of it, under conditions of uncertainty, as the "Numbers Trump Ability Theorem"* (Landemore 2013,

104; further clarified in Landemore 2014a, 188)[10]. Under conditions of uncertainty, the best proxy for cognitive diversity is full inclusiveness or, short of that (to make deliberation feasible), random selection.

If it is impossible to know ahead of time whom to include or exclude and if one speculates based on political tests, or tarot-reading for that matter, we might get it very wrong! It is pure hubris to assume that we can predict ahead of time which voices will matter or not in the future based on some political literacy tests designed by social scientists.

Concretely speaking, consider the cost to American politics of excluding the voices of poor, uneducated Blacks (the most likely victims of Brennan's exclusion by his admission). Indeed, we have already experienced the social cost of this exclusion. Given the patterns of exclusion of Black people in city politics, especially around policing, we have ended up with years of abuse by the police and systemic racism, on top of unrecognized white privilege from the top to the bottom of society. In this moment of racial reckoning, trying to establish as evident a fact as the existence of white privilege and as simple a moral truth as "Black Lives Matter" is still an uphill battle. At this point, regardless of political literacy on general political issues, how are the voices of Black citizens, and especially those of the women among them, not more informed, more useful, and thus more needed than those of almost anyone else on a number of social and political issue? In other words, aren't the voices of the 5% so casually excluded by Brennan

10. See also supra p. 17.

in the name of epistemic competence precisely more epistemically valuable, at this moment in history, than the other 95%?

Perhaps Brennan could reply that we do not need those voices because well-intentioned, well-informed liberals (like him!) understand the racial dimensions of social and economic inequality much better than do any of the 5% he excluded. He may believe that informed people should work on fixing the socioeconomic background conditions responsible for the racially skewed epistemic exclusions until we can educate the 5% back into the civic fold.

To this, I can only reply by directing him to a whole literature in standpoint epistemology that tells us that there is a limit to what any one of us can understand, even with empathy and curiosity, about the circumstances of any other differently "situated" being (e.g., Anderson 2017, Collins 1990, Hardin 1998, Medina 2013). Conversely, knowledge is always in part defined and colored by one's local, personal, biological, racial, gendered, historical, and otherwise differentiated place in the world. Knowledge, including political knowledge, is not a purely theoretical but also an experiential category. Du Bois applied this reasoning to the gender line as well as the color line: "With the best will and knowledge, no man can know women's wants as well as women themselves. To disenfranchise women is deliberately to turn from knowledge and grope in ignorance" (Du Bois 1999 [1920]: 84). He wrote this even as he recognized that inclusion would come at some epistemic cost as well, since those who bring much-needed perspectives on some topics may also bring ignorance on other topics with them.

Miranda Fricker's work on epistemic injustice (Fricker 2007) suggests that phenomena such as "sexual harassment," which correspond to a widespread female experience, cannot be recognized, labeled, and therefore addressed and properly punished as long as women are excluded from the places where human experiences are made sense of and legislated about. This type of "hermeneutical injustice"—the lack of recognition of a perspective on the world due to structural social prejudices—is the price we pay for the lack of political inclusion, not just with respect to women but also to all marginalized groups.

There is also an epistemic asymmetry between the privileged and the oppressed, the powerful and the powerless. Women arguably understand men better than men understand women. Blacks arguably understand whites better than whites can understand Blacks. As Baldwin put it, whereas the masters can ignore and look away from the slaves, the slaves have to face and learn to understand their masters. For this reason, Du Bois believed that the only person who could legitimately claim to represent us all was the most "damned" in our midst, namely Black women, whom he saw as carrying the burden, but also, the intimate knowledge of, several forms of oppression and their intersection: white supremacy and male patriarchy (he left out other dimensions of oppression having to do with sexual orientation). Because of their historical condition, Black women, he argued, have knowledge that no one else has.

So how ironic would it be, in a moment like this, to silence the very voices that our polity needs the most in order to learn about its failures and hopefully to fix them, learn, and heal?

Or consider the case of aboriginal tribes in Australia. By the standard of Brennan's political literacy test, it is not hard to guess that they would be excluded from his majoritarian epistocracy. The wildfires of 2019 destroyed entire ecosystems, over a billion animal lives, and too many human lives. In the wake of such a disaster, many argued that Australia should return to the Aboriginal practice of preventative partial burnings of the bush, which an increasingly technocratic state, dismissive or ignorant of indigenous knowledge, had criminalized as arson a few decades ago. Political knowledge is a living thing and comes in various guises. We should be humble about who has it and about the possibility of defining or identifying it ex ante.

Consider finally the case of the Yellow Vests in France, those peri-urban lower-class workers, many of them single mothers barely making ends meet, who rebelled against the Macron government's seemingly innocuous fuel tax. These people have so little voice in the French system that they felt the need to wear a neon yellow jacket and to demonstrate loudly in order to be seen and heard. Like poor Blacks in the US, many participants in the Yellow Vest movement are effectively excluded from electoral politics, even without official disenfranchisement. Electoral democracies, it turns out, are already very much like the partial epistocracies wanted by Brennan (see more on this below). Why is it bad for the system that such voices were not heard before? That their votes never really counted? It is bad because when the system fails to represent the interests and views of such people, it is likely to harm them or fail to help adequately. Moreover, the system may fail to anticipate the possibly violent reactions that the policies decided without their input will cause.

I take these examples because they correspond to the people most likely to be disenfranchised under Brennan's scheme. However, consider privileged citizens—white male libertarian philosophy professors or neo-liberal economists. Over the past few decades both groups have completely oversold open borders and free trade, the benefits of deregulation and liberalized markets, and they have failed to anticipate climate change. (This is meant as friendly banter, but I hope Brennan can acknowledge it contains a kernel of truth.) What would we lose if we excluded such people from public conversations and democratic voting? Not much, many people would say. Nevertheless, I would argue, we cannot afford to lose even such voices, not because they were right before (they were not), nor because they are particularly useful or relevant at the moment, but because they might become so again, tomorrow or the day after.

Ultimately, we cannot afford to lose a single voice, in the short or the long term. Any exclusion could prove epistemically costly at any point and will most likely prove so over the long term. Most importantly, there is no reason to exclude any voice in a model that assumes democratic deliberation itself can weed out the bad input.

There are many more arguments, of course, against the epistemic exclusion of the kind that Brennan would accept. One reason is the moral and psychological damage that exclusion does to the excluded, as well as to their children and community, in terms of self-respect, dignity, and autonomy. I will not use these obvious objections here since I aimed to answer Brennan within the purely instrumental parameters we set for this conversation. Nevertheless they carry the day if my argument alone cannot, not least because of the long-term epistemic consequences of such psychological damage.

As W. E. B. Du Bois reminds us, the question of political exclusion is always the same.

> Who may be excluded from a share in the ruling of men?
> Time and again the world has answered:
>> The ignorant
>> The inexperienced
>> The guarded
>> The unwilling
> That is, we have assumed that only the intelligent should vote, or those who know how to rule men, or those who are not under benevolent guardianship, or those who ardently desire the right.

This assumption that only the knowledgeable or intelligence should rule has been disproved many times over. With the enfranchisement of the poor, Black people, and women, society did not collapse. It improved. The answer to the question of who should rule has always been "all of us" because the relevant knowledge is tracked and produced by all of us coming together, as Protagoras already knew, Aristotle grudgingly acknowledged, and Du Bois insisted. As he put it with unmatched eloquence: "The vast and wonderful knowledge of this universe is locked in the bosoms of its individual souls. To tap this mighty reservoir of experience, knowledge, beauty, love, and deed we must appeal not to the few, not to some souls, but to all" (Du Bois 1999: 84).

Brennan's alternative to electoral democracy—plural voting and/or restricted franchise combined with a more important role for experts—does not qualify as "epistocracy" in the oligarchic sense. Nevertheless, it is an exclusionary form of democracy, of the type we have left behind with good reason. Even for specific questions put to the public, like referenda, the epistemic benefits of excluding the least competent, howsoever defined, are never worth the costs of sacrificing our commitment to political equality. The real danger is mistakenly eliminating what could be, in fact, the most relevant voices.

Chapter 8

If Democracy Is Such a Smart Regime, Why Are Democracies Doing So Poorly at the Moment and How Can We Fix Them?

IN PREVIOUS CHAPTERS I SPENT A lot of time refuting objections to the epistemic argument for democracy and arguments for epistocracy. However, if democracies are, in theory, epistemically superior to epistocracies, why are the regimes we conventionally call democracies in such crisis right now? Here is where I, perhaps surprisingly, concur with Brennan. Like him, I do not think that existing democracies are very functional. But, unlike Brennan, I argue that their dysfunctionality is a consequence of the fact that they are not democratic enough, that is, fail to sufficiently include and empower their citizens. Therefore, the way to fix them and to improve their epistemic value is by making them more inclusive and egalitarian, and indeed more open to the input of ordinary citizens. In the first section, I explain why I think current democracies are

Debating Democracy. Jason Brennan and Hélène Landemore, Oxford University Press. © Oxford University Press 2022. DOI: 10.1093/oso/9780197540817.003.0010

not democratic enough. In the second section I develop an alternative model of democracy that I call open democracy. In the third section I provide examples to illustrate what such an open democracy would look like. In the fourth section I consider some potential worries and objections, especially those having to do with the lack of electoral accountability in a fully open democratic system.

THE PROBLEM WITH ELECTORAL DEMOCRACY

Democracy, one might recall, means "people's power." Yet in our contemporary democracies it is not clear that the people have that much power. Representative government, the ancestor of our modern democracies, was born in the eighteenth century as a liberal-republican rather than democratic construct, primarily oriented toward the protection of certain individual rights rather than the empowerment of citizens per se. By "liberal" I mean here an ideology primarily concerned with protecting the inalienable rights of individuals against the encroachment of governments, including popular governments. By "republican," I mean an ideology where the ideal of non-domination of the individual trumps the ideal of popular rule (though these two ideals can perhaps be reconciled).[1] The prioritization of liberal-republican commitments and goals over purely democratic ones was compatible with giving the people

1. See the excellent volume by Elazar and Rousselière (2019) for an exploration of the complex historical and conceptual relationships between republicanism and democracy.

some say over the choice of rulers, a huge improvement over the regimes that came before. However, giving people a choice over their rulers did not translate automatically into popular rule. Representative government has in fact historically consisted of privileging the idea of people's *consent* to power over that of people's *exercise* of power.

The American Founders, for example, famously claimed to want to create a republic, as opposed to a democracy, which they associated with mob rule. James Madison, in particular, feared the tyranny of the majority as much as he disliked and rejected the old monarchical orders.[2] He wanted to create a mixed regime that would protect individuals not only from powerful minorities but also from oppressive majorities. Most importantly for Madison, the American republic would be characterized, in contrast to ancient democracies, by "the total exclusion of the people in its collective capacity from any share in [the government of the republic]" (Hamilton, Madison and Jay 2008, 63). The founders thus explicitly presented as a superior feature of their intended republic the fact that it was not meant to rest on *demos-kratos*, or people's power, but instead on the power of elected elites, itself properly limited by the division of power and a complex system of checks and balances.

Our modern democracies have inherited from these origins a congenital fear and lack of openness to citizen

2. For arguments to the contrary, see de Djinn (2019) to the effect that Madison, far from being a mere liberal or a liberal republican, was in fact an authentically democratic republican with the utmost respect for the majoritarian principle. See also Tuck 2016.

participation as well as a problematic adherence to an elitist conception of representation as best performed by elected officials. The Federalists thus aimed to staff representative assemblies with a natural aristocracy of talent and wisdom capable of enlarging and refining common people's views (Madison, *Federalist* 10). They privileged a vision of representation as a "filter" primarily seeking to maximize the average competence of the representatives while accepting the costs of reducing their group to a sociologically and economically homogeneous group of people. But as we saw earlier this view of what makes for smart deliberative assemblies in politics is not only dated, it is likely wrong, if it is indeed true that the diversity of the group is more important than the individual competence of its members.

Interestingly, there was a competing theory of democratic representation available in the 18th century. The Anti-Federalists (Melancton Smith in particular, taking up ideas put forward by John Adams) favored an ideal regime closer to the direct democracy so scorned by their opponents and which they saw successfully implemented in the contemporary Swiss confederacy, of comparable size, population, and wealth as the U.S. Short of directly democratic institutions, they envisaged as a second-best an ideal of representation as "mirror" or "miniature portrait of the people" (Adams [1776] 1856: 193). They argued that only people with at least a number of similar traits and lived-experience could properly speak on behalf of common people and, indeed, have the relevant political knowledge. Whether they realized it or not, their model privileged the reproduction on the small scale of the diversity of the entire citizenry and was much less concerned with the competence of individual representatives.

Why did the Anti-Federalists, who anticipated some of the contemporary ideas about the factors of collective intelligence and the benefits of cognitive diversity, lose the battle of ideas in the 18th century? One of the many reasons is the ideological dominance of elections as the marker and carrier of political legitimacy. As Manin describes it, elections in the 18th century "triumphed" over any other alternative selection method (including the obvious democratic alternative of lotteries) because of the theory of political legitimacy that was dominant at the time, which linked legitimacy to consent (since the 17th century social contract theory) and, specifically, consent at the ballot booth (Manin 1997: 67-93). As a result, the Anti-Federalists could only imagine selecting representatives by election, which is not a method suited to producing a "mirror-image" of the nation. The Anti-Federalists' solution to this problem was to plead for smaller constituencies and a larger number of representatives, hoping that these conditions would generate assemblies at least representative of the middle-class rather than just the "natural aristocracy" of the country. But this second-best solution of course, which had other problems of its own, failed to convince. By contrast the idea of representation as a filter and the practice of elections as selecting the more competent from among the citizenry were a perfect conceptual and ideological fit.

The next historical step in the evolution of representative governments was to go from parliamentary democracy—where the legislative assembly is seen as a place of deliberation among individually superior minds—to party democracy. Now, the entire public sphere, including the formal one, became a competition between policy platforms that individual citizens or their representatives adjudicate between via voting.

Representative government, from its early elitist beginnings to today's partisan version, also corresponds to a dated understanding of what makes groups smart and the civic virtues one should cultivate in both leaders and citizens to foster collective intelligence in politics. Elections of representatives, in particular, present several problems from a democratic point of view. They are by nature an ambiguously democratic selection mechanism, creating and thriving off inequalities between people. They do not mesh well with the seemingly valuable ideals of deliberation and open-mindedness put forward by deliberative democrats over the last thirty years. And they do not produce enough of the diversity needed for good decision-making. As such, we may legitimately see elections as preventing rather than facilitating genuine rule by the people.

The democratic deficits at the heart of representative democracy are sufficiently severe to account for at least part of its current institutional crisis. Perhaps other factors, such as globalization, capitalism, and technology, as well as the economic inequalities they entail, made things worse, but the fragility is in the initial design.

OPEN DEMOCRACY

Let us now assume that we could design democracy from scratch, rather than evolving it from the current versions with which we are familiar. Furthermore, let us assume that we want to maximize its epistemic value. What would such a democracy look like? I assume here that we would still need a form of democratic representation so that a sufficiently small number of individuals in our midst can deliberate (since to this day we do not know how to conduct quality mass deliberation).

If the argument presented in chapter 4 is correct, what matters for the epistemic reliability of deliberations among democratic representatives is that their group be cognitively diverse rather than made up of individually smart but cognitively homogenous people. From this point of view, elections are not an optimal way of selecting representatives because even under ideal conditions, they rely on a "principle of distinction" (Manin 1997). That is, elections discriminate against those who cannot stand out socially in the eyes of others. As a result, elections cannot be fully reconciled with the goal of maximal cognitive diversity. The persons most likely to run for office are likely to share some personality traits (type-A personalities, say), or other homogenous characteristics that may reduce the overall cognitive diversity of the assembly. As a consequence, even if the individual ability of the members of such elected assemblies is high, their cognitive diversity will not be as high as it could be.

Assuming that, on average, the citizens from among whom we select representatives meet a minimal threshold of individual competence, random selection is a more promising, authentically democratic way of selecting representatives that maximizes cognitive diversity in the face of political uncertainty. Random selection, performed through "civic lotteries," for example, would in the ideal produce what is known as "descriptive representation" of the people (Pitkin 1967), or in Charles Adams's famous formula, "an exact portrait, in miniature, of the people at large"

(Adams 185, 194–195). That is, it would ensure a statistical similarity of thoughts and preferences between the rulers and the ruled. Many scholars have studied random selection as an alternative to elections on many grounds: equality, fairness, representativeness, anti-corruption potential, protection against conflict and domination, avoidance of preference aggregation problems, and cost-effectiveness, among others (e.g., Elster 1989, 78–103; Mulgan 1984, 539–560; Goodwin 1992; Carson and Martin 1999; Duxbury 1999; Stone 2007, 2009, 2011; Sintomer 2007; Guerrero 2014; Abizadeh 2019). The descriptive representation that lotteries would achieve is normatively desirable for specifically epistemic reasons as well. Descriptive representation achieved through random selection would not elevate the level of individual ability in the deliberative assembly, as by definition the expected individual ability of the selected individuals would be average. However, it would preserve the cognitive diversity of the larger group. Thus, besides its other possible advantages, random selection holds the promise of improving the epistemic quality of deliberation among representatives.

Note another implication of the argument presented at the beginning of this essay: no matter how we select the subset of deliberators from the broader population, whether by election or by random lotteries, those selected should not stay in power forever. A regular turnover of representatives seems like a minimal requirement if the goal is to inject and maintain some cognitive diversity over the long term. Even if the turnover were limited to a specific subset of the population (the more educated, say), at least it would solve the problem of ossifying oligarchies, whose members end up thinking the same way as one another and losing sight of the common good. Terms of limited length—already an essential and uncontroversial feature of representative government (Manin 1997)—and terms of limited number—accepted for offices such as the presidency, but not for legislators—thus seem like an important guarantee of the minimal cognitive diversity of the decision-making body over the long term.

What would it look like to have a democracy based on the choice of democratic representatives by random selection? In a recent book (Landemore 2020), I have explored this question and argued that five main institutional principles structure open democracy. These five principles are participation rights, deliberation, majority rule, democratic representation, and transparency.

Rather than examining each principle in the abstract, let me paint a portrait of open democracy, which should appear both quite familiar and strikingly different. From a practical point of view, open democracy might still include a lot of institutions we are familiar with such as an elected executive and an appointed Supreme Court. We may maintain the plausible principle of a separation of powers, which has to do with a practical belief in the merits of a division of labor and the virtues of power checking power. However, legislative power, which is my main focus here, would lay in the hands of ordinary citizens rather than elected officials at all levels of the polity. Like ancient democracy, open democracy would thus be mostly run by what I call "lottocratic" representatives selected through civic lotteries.[3]

---

3. Additionally, and unlike in the mixed regime that we are familiar with in the US, ultimate legislative authority would lie with the people, as opposed to the Supreme Court.

In open democracy, a nationwide network of such randomly selected legislative bodies would work in parallel and, when relevant, in a connected way, with the lower-level assemblies feeding the deliberations of the ones at higher levels. The multiplication of such bodies would ensure that, from bottom to top, the polity's deliberations are continually refreshed by the influx of frequently rotated, diverse and as statistically representative as possible samples of the population, incorporating all of the perspectives, ideas, and information needed to guide the ship of state in the right direction.

But what if incompetent people filled these assemblies, an objector might object. A concern with random selection is that this mode of selection would one day lead to the appointment of extremely incompetent and/or morally corrupt individuals (e.g., Nazis or white supremacists) who would cause serious problems (epistemic and otherwise). Over time, indeed, under a continuous system of unrestricted random sampling, the probability of such an unlucky draw goes to 1. This is, however, an almost purely theoretical concern. In a previous publication, I calculated that in order for chance to staff a small assembly of fifty people with a majority of, say, terribly incompetent and evil people, assuming that 25% of the larger population

> While a Supreme Court would thus still play a crucial role as a check on majorities gone awry, there should be a way for citizens to initiate a recall referendum on a Supreme Court decision they deem sufficiently unjust (on the existing Swiss model). The procedural constraints on such a process would be such as to minimize the frequency of recourse to such a recall option while preserving the inherently democratic principle of popular sovereignty.

consists of these incompetent and evil people, the probability would be 0.0038% (Landemore 2012). For the probability to rise to 50% (renewing the assembly every four years), it would take 72,924 years. For the risk to rise to 1%, it would take 1,060 years. Most assemblies are much larger than fifty people. Additionally, no democracy has lived that long, and at least some representative democracies based on the election principle have managed to produce much worse assemblies in much shorter periods. We could indeed be unlucky and, against the odds, draw the dangerous assembly on the first trial or soon thereafter. In a well-designed democracy, however, there should be institutional safeguards that limit the damage that could be caused by a particularly bad, if unlikely, draw. Constitutional checks and the existence of a second, non-randomly selected chamber, for example, may come to mind. All in all, the risks associated with random sampling do not appear sufficiently significant to justify rejecting the procedure.[4]

Empirical evidence backs up the prediction that under some non-exacting conditions, groups of average citizens perform decently well when placed in the right deliberative conditions. Deliberative Polls or Citizens' Assemblies, which gather between 100 and 500 randomly or quasi-randomly selected participants, seem to offer such deliberative conditions. Deliberative Polls, despite lasting two or fewer days, provide participants with briefing material that they can discuss in smaller groups of fifteen or so, as well as access to expert panels that they can question at length during plenary sessions. Citizens' Assemblies, which have

---

4. For a refutation of the same objection along similar lines, see Mueller et al. 2011, 54.

a longer lifespan of several weeks to several months, allow for even more in-depth pre-deliberation reading and processing of information while facilitating deliberation over the course of many meetings. Both kinds of groups produce epistemically promising outcomes. Deliberative Polls produce more informed post-deliberation preferences on topics ranging from the selection of a candidate for mayor in the 2006 Deliberation Poll organized in Greece, to the choice of energy policies in American Deliberative Polls, to the reform of the European Union pension system in the 2007 Deliberative Poll called "Tomorrow's Europe" (see Fishkin 2009). The 2004 British Columbia Citizens' Assembly produced, over several months, a sophisticated and innovative proposal on the complex topic of electoral reform, meant to address the problem of democratic deficits in Canada (Warren and Pearse 2008). The recent French Citizen Convention for Climate, which included 150 randomly selected citizens, produced, with the help of around 130 experts put at their service, high-quality law-like proposals, some of which went on to be directly turned into regulation. The size of such experiments, involving a little more than 100 people in the case of Citizens' Assemblies and up to 500 in the case of Deliberative Polls, is sufficiently large to make the random selected bodies close to genuinely representative. We can also extrapolate from the performance of regular citizens in these deliberative contexts to the expected performance of a randomly selected parliament, which is likely to be of a similar size. The results of these experiments should also assuage the fear that increased communication costs offset the benefits of cognitive diversity in a randomly selected representative assembly. Deliberative Polls, in particular, have been a success across the globe, sometimes despite challenging communicative contexts induced by language barriers, cultural differences, and even profound value rifts, as in the case of the 2007 Deliberative Poll in Northern Ireland involving Protestants and Catholics (see Fishkin 2009, 159–169 and also Farrar et al. 2010). The OECD (Organisation for Economic Co-operation and Development) has recently documented the "deliberative wave" of mini-publics that have taken place in OECD countries in recent decades. They documented around 289 cases of such deliberative bodies of randomly selected citizens, the vast majority of which yielded positive results.

Scholars have pointed out that the epistemic failures of deliberation in some instances can lead to group polarization rather than to any form of epistemically sound consensus (e.g., Sunstein 2002). These failures are vastly exaggerated. In the end, the empirical literature on deliberation yields, at worst, mixed or inconclusive results (e.g., Thompson 2008, 499–500 but see Curato et al. 2017 for more optimistic claims). The negative results observed in some deliberative contexts can be explained not by a failure of deliberation per se, but rather by a failure at implementing the minimal conditions under which deliberation can take place at all. These conditions include setting up the deliberation as a truly argumentative form of exchange among diverse individuals, which guarantees that individuals' confirmation biases check rather than reinforce one another (see Mercier and Landemore 2012; Mercier and Sperber 2011). The evidence garnered against deliberation generally comes from groups of like-minded people who never end up engaging one another's arguments in an appropriately deliberative manner (see also Manin 2005).

How would such randomly selected assemblies be able to rule themselves, and in particular set an agenda for themselves, absent the party hierarchies and party discipline that help structure existing parliamentary debates? Wouldn't ordinary citizens find themselves in what Gary Cox (2008) calls "the legislative state of nature" in which the freedom of all to speak at any time on anything would quickly devolve into anarchy and chaos?

One can surmise that lottocratic assemblies would have to choose a governing committee of sorts headed by one or several chairs to impose some rule and order on the proceedings of the assembly. The governance committee could, for example, be selected by lot and frequently rotated as well. Additionally, there would have to be some procedural rules and protocols, perhaps summarized in a document like Robert's Rules of Order, to ensure that deliberation among several hundred or at least dozens of people (depending on the size of such bodies) does not turn into chaos. However, if the Ancient Greeks could run a large city using assemblies of 500 to 1000 people, we can surely do so today. Several organizational models have been put in practice in the dozens of largely successful Citizens' Assemblies conducted around the world since the 1980s. For the most part, external organizers and agencies under the control of the existing government or some other organization have organized these assemblies. In the case of the recent French Convention for Climate, for example, the specific agenda—to write up laws or legal proposals to help curb carbon emissions in a spirit of social justice—was set by the French executive. An independently appointed Governance Committee of fifteen people framed the specific agenda of each session and the structure of the weekend meetings of the 150 members. From the second meeting onward, the Governance committee included two randomly selected representatives of the citizens themselves, rotating from session to session. The committee drew upon the expert advice of the social entrepreneurs in charge of facilitating the meetings as well as the feedback and specific requests of the 150 citizens (as channeled through their representatives on the Governance Committee). The current models are, of course, problematic because they arguably give too much power to external authorities and independent agencies, raising the question of agenda-manipulation. Ideally, as we move toward the actual institutionalization of such citizens' bodies, new models will be designed to give more autonomy and control to the members while preserving the conditions for order and good deliberation. There is no reason to think that these questions of internal governance and procedural organization cannot be resolved in ways that are both theoretically and empirically satisfactory.

In open democracy, lottocratic assemblies would function in an organic and fluid relationship with the rest of the public. Lottocratic representatives would need to connect to the rest of the citizenry via crowdsourcing platforms generating ideas. Most importantly the availability of citizens' initiatives and rights of referral would make it possible for sufficiently motivated minorities gathering enough signatures to trigger nation-wide referenda on new citizen-initiated proposals or on existing laws that seem problematic to a significant fraction of the population. Top-down referenda initiated by official institutions or planned as part of the legislative process could allow the larger public to have a say on the work of their lottocratic representatives. In the end, the most striking feature of this new kind of democracy is that there might not be any elected assemblies in it. However, there might still be elected committees and councils. For example, one welcome change to the executive function could be to replace the model of the lone presidential figure with a council of several people, as in Switzerland (where the executive consists of seven ministers who rotate for one year in the function of president for purposes of foreign representation). Going one step further, one may also want to curb the least democratic powers (the executive and the judicial powers) through other means than competition with the legislative assemblies; for example, by limiting the powers of the executive and allowing the direct will of the citizens to initiate and determine constitutional changes at the federal level (another interesting feature of Swiss democracy).

Open democracy is thus a vision of politics that returns power to ordinary citizens and in which politics remains, proudly, an amateur's sport. The view of politicians as a separate caste of knowers is not a part of open democracy. This is not to say, however, that there is no room for professionals and experts in an open democracy. Expert administrators, expert advisors, and lawyers will still have roles to play in supporting and informing the work of randomly selected assemblies (functions that they already perform in relation to the members of elected legislatures). As we saw with the case of French Citizens' Convention for Climate, the role of supporting administration and expert advice is crucial to the quality of the deliberations within lottocratic bodies. However, the law should ultimately be initiated, inspired, supervised, shaped, vetted, and ultimately *made* by ordinary citizens, not career politicians, let alone experts.

A purely non-electoral model of open democracy is probably unrealistic for existing democracies. However, it could be implemented from scratch in new communities, including digital communities like the "cloud nations" of e-Estonia and Bitnation, agglomerates of existing institutions (e.g., merged firms, hospitals, colleges), and perhaps even countries seeking to transition to democracy while leap-frogging the historical paradigm of electoral democracy. Even where it proves unfeasible in its pure form, this ideal blueprint gives us a sense of the direction that we should head toward if we want to democratize our institutions further.

Realistically, we probably have to evolve existing institutions from where they are. In existing democracies, the most plausible scenario is the addition of a new chamber alongside the existing set of constitutionally entrenched legislative assemblies. This new body could be called the Chamber of Participation, the People's House, or the Chamber for the Future. In some cases it may be worth considering the replacement of an existing chamber. Abizadeh (2019) suggests replacing the notoriously dysfunctional Canadian Senate with a chamber selected by lot. In France, a law was recently passed to turn our third legislative chamber (the Economic, Social and Environmental Council, or CESE in French) into the Chamber of citizens' conventions (though in practice the changes are much less radical and ambitious than the new name suggests). The primary function of such a new chamber, in current schemes, would be to generate an agenda, relative to one or several sets of issues for the elected legislature (Gastil and Wright 2019; Landemore 2020). The elected legislature would be constrained, legally, to study, address, and answer the proposal(s) of the Citizens' Assemblies. This hybrid model would allow for inclusive agenda-setting while preserving a role for elected officials. The preservation of a central legislative role for elected representatives can be justified on the grounds of the know-how of existing elected representatives. Incumbents have institutional memory about the failure of similar reforms in the past, technical knowledge of the way that legal statutes are supposed to be written, and practical knowledge of the likely reactions to a law once it is passed. One may thus want to limit the role of randomly selected chambers to the function of agenda-setting at a general level or perhaps that of dealing with a limited set of issues.

Let me consider, however, the case for granting the randomly selected chamber a more ambitious legislative role, that of actually making the law, at least on the set of issues that the agenda-setting chamber is given jurisdiction over. I remain agnostic for now as to whether the same set of randomly selected citizens should both set the agenda and write the laws or whether one should divide the labor involved in these different stages of the process between different batches of randomly selected citizens.

Note that while the arguments above about the expertise of traditional elected law-makers make sense in theory, the reality is very different. Much of the writing of the law in elected parliaments is outsourced to committees where lobbyists and lawyers wield enormous power and influence. This is perhaps as it should be, given the complexity of the legal codes and international treatises to which national law must conform. However, there is no reason to think that lottocratic representatives would be less capable than elected representatives of performing the task of limited outsourcing. In general, whatever prudential knowledge elected legislators may have accumulated over the years must be traded off against the cognitive homogeneity and close-mindedness that such experience fosters. On balance, it is not clear that the advantages of political experience outweigh its drawbacks in comparison to the performance of more novice representatives.

For example, there might be a reasonable fear that inexperienced citizens would be less able than veteran elected representatives to scrutinize the work of committees and keep the experts on them accountable. But one could argue that the energy and enthusiasm of beginners might at least partly compensate for their lack of experience. Meanwhile, elected representatives, especially if they have been in power for decades, may have become too complacent or too cozy with the experts and lobbyists that they recruit to write the law for them. Empirically, there is currently little to no data to compare the relative performance of the two types of legislators. The case of the French Convention for Climate, however, suggests that randomly selected citizens working closely with legal counsels to produce law-like proposals are not as deferential and manipulable as one might suspect. Perhaps precisely because they have not developed long-lasting relationships with experts, they prove to be fierce guardians of their sovereignty over the texts and have shown that, when given the power and the means, they know how to keep experts on tap and themselves on top.

Still, the objector might ask, in a pure model of open, non-electoral democracy, how would we keep unelected representatives accountable to the people if we do not have the sanctioning mechanism of elections? In a more hybrid model, wouldn't the presence of a new, unelected agenda-setting and possibly partly legislative chamber disrupt electoral accountability by forcing legislators to address issues that may not have been on their campaign platforms?

These are natural questions that I partly address in my book (Landemore 2020). I argue that, at least in theory, a democratic system can achieve many, perhaps even all of the things we expect from a broad notion of "accountability"—the giving of reasons, the capacity to sanction retroactively, the capacity to prevent corruption and promote good behavior—without electoral mechanisms. Electoral mechanisms, I contend, are not as essential to political accountability as is generally assumed. They are neither the only sources of political accountability nor necessarily the best mechanisms to generate it.

First of all, in terms of accountability *stricto sensu*, it is not clear that elections foster all that much by way of justification of politicians' chosen actions and policies. When they seek power, electoral candidates make promises, which are not accounts. When they seek reelection, one would expect them to give accounts, explaining and justifying their past choices and the reasons why they think their policies were validated or at least understandable in retrospect. But even as some of that account-giving takes place, political campaigns are as much a time for spin, manipulation, and strategic lies as for genuine engagement with reasons and arguments.

As to the "sanctioning" value of elections, it is in doubt among political scientists themselves. According to James Fearon, for example, elections are not about holding governments to account (i.e., here, sanctioning them) but instead about choosing good governments. They are about selection rather than sanction per se. Among other reasons, he points out that if elections were purely about sanctions, then the existence of term limits would in many cases render elections entirely ineffectual. Fearon thus suggests that elections are more plausibly seen as a future-oriented device to select the right kind of political leaders and representatives (Fearon 1999). Even in theory, it is hard to see elections as more than an extraordinarily imperfect and blunt tool for sanctioning elected officials. As Ferejohn and Rosenbluth remark, "Elections, the typical way of disciplining political agents, are a crude and imperfect way to control officials; they happen infrequently and they can usually only punish or reward officials by withholding or awarding office" (2009, 273).

More importantly, however, elections are not the only mechanism that may induce governments in a democracy, representative or open, to give accounts for their actions and to act in responsible ways.

Evidence for this bold claim comes, first, from Ancient Athens. The Greeks had various non-electoral mechanisms, from popular juries and the vetting of candidates for office to the practice of *euthynai* (the giving of accounts at the end of one's stint in government), as well as the practice of ostracism and later the *graphe paranomon*, all of which kept decision-makers in check. All of these practices and institutions served as accountability mechanisms in a broad sense and, as far as we can tell, worked reasonably well. They were probably overly strict and punitive, in that Ancient Athenians were held accountable for their proposals, not just their actions. Decision-makers could be punished for sheer bad luck, regardless of whether they had been demonstrably incompetent or dishonest (Elster 1999). At any rate, the Athenian example suggests that a lack of accountability need not be an issue even for a system where elections play no role or a lesser one.

Finally, there are other internal accountability mechanisms to an open democracy that I explore in my book, including participatory rights, deliberation, and transparency. In addition to these institutional features of open democracy, one may also count on the individual psychological mechanisms that presumably already play at least some role in elected assemblies, such as a sense of honor or duty or even the fraternity and solidarity felt for one's fellow citizens. Honor and duty would arguably play even more of a role in non-electoral contexts since in electoral democracies partisanship and the need to win power at any cost are often used as excuses to override virtues seen as outdated. Electoral and partisan incentives may indeed undermine rather than promote feelings of identification and belonging.

Finally, we might need special ethics committees to audit the functioning of non-electoral assemblies and the behavior of their members to make sure that nothing untoward occurs, such as misappropriation or misuse of public funds, systematic lying or spreading of misinformation during debates, intimidation or corruption of other members, abuses of power, and moral or sexual harassment. The special ethics committees could be composed like a citizen's jury, at random, or chosen from among former lottocratic or self-selected representatives with particularly good reputations. These ethics committee would not necessarily be different from current ethics committees staffed by members of the legislature or law enforcement agencies.

Just as we are accustomed to thinking about representation in electoral terms, so we are also used to thinking of political accountability in exclusively electoral contexts. This makes us overly sensitive to the lack of electoral mechanisms in open democracy. Nevertheless, elections are not a definitional element of political accountability. They are at most one possible mechanism for achieving it. In other words, elections are one way of causing the relationship of accountability between rulers and ruled to obtain. In an open democracy where elections would play less of a prominent role, one should not expect the usual mechanisms to causally obtain the relationship of accountability. But there is no reason to think that it could not be secured through other channels.

CONCLUSION

I have argued that democracy, defined as a regime characterized by an inclusive and egalitarian decision procedure, is epistemically superior to epistocracy, a regime that limits the number of people included in the decision process or weights their voices and votes unequally. Note that throughout this essay, I have not deployed what is perhaps the easiest argument against epistocracy, the argument from corruption. I assume throughout, rather generously, that this problem is not more prevalent among epistocracies than democracies. Nor have I emphasized the moral shortcomings of epistocracy: namely, that it compromises what I assume is our shared commitment to equality and autonomy.

In the end, I believe that there are three instrumental arguments against advocates of epistocracy or meritocracy at the theoretical level. I have only explored the first of these three in this essay. They are as follows:

> 1. Democracy is more likely to identify problems and to fig-
> ure out solutions to them at any point in time (because its
> inclusiveness brings in more cognitive diversity whatever
> the issue).

Because its legislators are more representative of the vast range of ideas and interests found in the larger population, democracy (especially of the open kind) is more likely than epistocracy to identify the most significant problems in society and the solutions to them. By contrast, elites trained in the same schools and selected according to relatively narrow criteria will produce a relatively homogenous elite of very smart people who do not think differently and will get stuck at lower optima. If it is the case that the group's problem-solving abilities are more dependent on its cognitive diversity than its members' individual competence (assuming meritocratic criteria do measure competence appropriately), then a meritocratic system will never be optimal at any point in time, whereas a democracy, through the sheer number of views it comes to represent, will. There is thus some merit to William F. Buckley's famous quip that "one would rather be governed by the first fifty names in the phone book than the Harvard faculty." The conservative's fear was that Harvard faculty was too liberal, tolerant, and too likely to disagree with his views on race. Others would fear the arrogance of intellectual elites. However, lack of cognitive diversity might be the real reason to worry about an Harvardocracy.

2. Democracy explores more of the political landscape over time (because of the renewal of political personnel).

The same argument gains even more traction when we look at the problem over time, longitudinally. We know from social science that, over time, groups tend to conform and polarize in the direction favored by the initial majority. Decision-making bodies that are not renewed sufficiently frequently will be particularly susceptible to groupthink and polarization. By contrast, in a system that renews the pool of political decision-makers frequently, there is a greater chance of avoiding these risks. Democracy's advantage lies both in its inclusiveness and in the fact that it periodically rotates its political personnel, sustaining and reproducing inclusiveness and diversity in the long run. As a result, over time, democracy based on periodic elections or some other mechanism ensuring frequent rotation of political personnel is likely to outperform a fixed meritocracy in its ability to identify problems and, more generally, track the truth. Of course, one could argue for a periodically rotated meritocracy. However, rotating meritocrats would only fix the second part of the problem. Considering the recent consolidation of power by Xi Jinping, it is also not clear that meritocracies can reliably maintain rotation.

3. Democracy has more ability for self-correction.

Finally, democracies will make mistakes. However, unlike epistocracies, they are incentivized to correct them quickly. The opponents of a decision that turns out to be bad for the country will be quickly empowered to revert it. Open democracies, especially, are more likely to be aware of the negative consequences of bad policies (or the absence of good policies), and thus more likely to correct them swiftly. By contrast, in an epistocracy that is not subject to the check of popular opinion, errors may persist a lot longer, with damaging consequences. Here again, a rotating epistocracy might be superior to a non-rotating one, but, again, rotation would only take care of half the problem.

These three arguments can be reduced to one: democracy is the better heuristic in the face of political uncertainty (about what the relevant problems are and what the appropriate responses should look like).

A last note. I'm putting the final touches to this text from my home at what appears to be the tail-end (in the US at least) of a pandemic which has in some ways been a giant social experiment to test the epistemic properties of regime forms around the world. When the dust settles, who will have addressed the pandemic "best" in the sense of having minimized the death toll while preserving fundamental rights and maintaining standards of social justice and the possibility for economic recovery, all relative to the country's initial conditions? And what will this say of the respective merits of democratic versus less democratic countries, but also centralized versus decentralized, small versus large, homogenous versus heterogenous countries?

For a while it seemed like democratic Taiwan and authoritarian Singapore were the role models while authoritarian Iran and democratic Italy were the worst-case scenarios. Meanwhile, China, the largest epistocracy on earth, successfully imposed massive quarantines on millions of people, built hospitals in eight days, and then, as the outbreak in China came slowly under control, sent millions of masks and expert teams around the world to help other countries. At the same time, China is responsible for mishandling the initial phase of its response to the pandemic with a state cover-up of the outbreak that ultimately wasted crucial time, doomed many lives, and irresponsibly contributed to making it all but inevitable that the virus would infect the rest of the world. On the other side of the world, one of the largest and oldest democracies, the United States of America, wasted precious weeks pretending that COVID-19 was nothing but a bad flu, proved incapable of containing or tracing the virus, or getting enough people to wear masks in public. Yet it is now leading the way in terms of vaccination speed.

All in all, the evidence seems to be that the countries with past experiences with pandemics or other traumatic events involving sacrifices of the population (like South Korea, Taiwan, and China with SARS and MERS and Greece with the economic crisis) did better than countries without such prior exposures. Others suggest that female leadership was key as New Zealand and Germany had in common a female prime minister. Others suggest that sometimes a pandemic is just a pandemic and that no regime is better equipped to deal with it per se. For others, it is still too soon to definitively conclude that democratic institutions gave some countries an advantage in the matter.

From my perspective, at any rate, it could be that democracies are worse at handling certain types of situations (including, perhaps, pandemics) while retaining an advantage overall in terms of handling constantly changing bundles of issues. Thus, even if it turned out that epistocratic regimes like China proved vastly superior to democratic regimes in the way they handled the pandemic (which is still in doubt), this would only prove their superiority over one particular issue, not across a diversity of issues. A judgment about the overall epistemic superiority of a regime cannot be made issue by issue. It must be made over all possible issues at once (though it is no doubt fair to weigh certain issues, such as a pandemic or national security, more heavily than others).

Note, finally, that even if real-life democracies were made sufficiently democratic, existing democracies would still suffer from various pathologies. Globalization has now shifted the levers of power from the nation-state to the international level, while empowering giant and oligarchically run international corporations that themselves dwarf and constrain the powers of national governments. In other words, the loss of state sovereignty in a globalized world can be blamed for a lot of the failings of existing democracies. The Trump election and Brexit, for example, suggest a clear trade-off between the loss of democratic sovereignty at the level of the nation-state and the gains of a more integrated world order. If the arguments I put forward stand, the weakness or nonexistence of authentically democratic institutions at the global level harms humankind as a whole, most centrally in the crisis of climate change.

REFERENCES

Abizadeh, Arash. 2019. "Representation, Bicameralism, Political Equality, and Sortition: Reconstituting the Second Chamber as a Randomly Selected Assembly," *Perspectives on Politics* 18(1): 1059–1078.

Acemoglu, Daron, Suresh Naidu, Pascual Restrepo, and James A. Robinson. 2018. "Democracy Does Cause Growth," *Journal of Political Economy* 127(1): 47–100.

Achen, Christopher, and Larry Bartels. 2016. *Democracy for Realists*. Princeton: Princeton University Press.

Adams, John. (1851) 1856. "Thoughts on Government." In *The Works of John Adams, Second President of the United States: With a Life of the Author, Notes and Illustrations, by His Grandson Charles Francis Adams*. Boston: Little, Brown and Co., 4. E-book available at http://oll.libertyfund.org/title/2102.

Althaus, Scott. 2003. *Collective Preferences in Democratic Politics: Opinion Surveys and the Will of the People*. Cambridge: Cambridge University Press.

Anderson, Elizabeth. 2006. "The Epistemology of Democracy." *Episteme: A Journal of Social Epistemology* 3(1-2): 8–22.

Anderson, Elizabeth. 2017. "Feminist Epistemology and Philosophy of Science." In E.N. Zalta, ed., *Stanford Encyclopedia of Philosophy*.

Ashworth, Scott, and Ethan Bueno de Mesquita. 2014. "Is Voter Competence Good for Voters? Information, Rationality, and Democratic Performance," *American Political Science Review* 108(3): 565–587.

Bell, Daniel A. 2015. *The China Model. Political Meritocracy and the Limits of Democracy.* Princeton: Princeton University Press.

Bell, Daniel A., and Chenyang Li, eds. 2013. *The East Asian Challenge for Democracy: Political Meritocracy in Comparative Perspective.* Cambridge: Cambridge University Press.

Berelson, Bernard R., Paul F. Lazarsfeld, and William N. McPhee. 1954. *Voting: A Study of Opinion Formation in a Presidential Campaign.* Chicago: University of Chicago Press.

Black, Duncan. 1958. *Theory of Elections and Committees.* Cambridge: Cambridge University Press.

Bovens, Luc, and Wlodek Rabinowicz. 2006. "Democratic Answers to Complex Questions—An Epistemic Perspective," *Synthese* 150(1): 131–153.

Brennan, Jason. 2016. *Against Democracy.* Princeton: Princeton University Press.

Brennan, Jason. 2014. "How Smart is Democracy? You Can't Answer that Question a Priori." *Critical Review: A Journal of Politics and Society* 26(1-2): 33–58.

Brennan, Jason. 2009. "Polluting the Polls: When Citizens Should Not Vote." *Australasian Journal of Philosophy* 87(4): 535–549.

Caplan, Bryan. 2007. *Why Democracies Choose Bad Policies.* Princeton: Princeton University Press.

Carson, Lyn, and Brian Martin. 1999. *Random Selection in Politics. (Luck of the Draw: Sortition and Public Policy).* Westport, CT: Praeger Publishers.

Cheng, Joseph Y.S., ed. 2011. *Whither China's Democracy? Democratization in China since the Tiananmen Incident.* Hong Kong: City University of Hong Kong Press.

Coleman, Matthew Benjamin. 2019. "Toward a Critical Theory of Technocracy: Power, Knowledge, and Elite Domination." Paper presented at the 2019 Convention of the American Political Science Association.

Collins, Patricia Hill. 1990. *Black Feminist Thought.* Boston: Unwin Hyman.

Converse, Philip E. 1990. "Popular Representation and the Distribution of Information." In J. A. Ferejohn and J. H. Kuklinski, eds., *Information and Democratic Processes.* Chicago: University of Illinois Press, 369–389.

Curato, Nicole, John S. Dryzek, Selen A. Ercan, Carolyn M. Hendriks, and Simon Niemeyer. 2017. "Twelve Key Findings in Deliberative Democracy Research," *Daedalus* 146(3): 14–38.

Curşeu, Petru Lucian, Rob J. G. Jansen, and Maryse M. H. Chappin. 2013. "Decision rules and group rationality." *PLoS ONE* 8(2): e56454.

Du Bois, W.E.B. 1999 [1920]. *Dark Water. Voices from within the veil.* Mineola, NY: Dover Publications.

Duxbury, Neil. 1999. *Random Justice: On Lotteries and Legal Decision-Making.* Oxford: Oxford University Press.

Elazar, Yiftah, and Geneviève Rousselière, eds. 2019. *Republicanism and the Future of Democracy.* Cambridge: Cambridge University Press.

Elster, Jon. 1989. "The Market and the Forum: Three Varieties of Political Theory." In J. Elster and A. Hylland, eds., *Foundations of Social Choice Theory.* Cambridge: Cambridge University Press, 104–132.

Elster, Jon. 1999. "Accountability in Athenian Politics." In A. Przeworski, S. C. Stokes, and B. Manin, eds., *Democracy, Accountability, and Representation.* Cambridge: Cambridge University Press, 253–278.

Elster, Jon and Hélène Landemore. 2018. "Philosophy of the Social Sciences," in A. Barberousse, D. Bonnay, and M. Cozic, *The Philosophy of Science: A Companion,* Oxford University Press.

Estlund, David. 2008. *Democratic Authority.* Princeton, NJ: Princeton University Press.

Estlund, David. 1997. "Beyond Fairness and Deliberation: The Epistemic Dimension of Democratic Authority." In James Bohman and William Rehg, eds., *Deliberative Democracy: Essays on Reason and Politics.* Cambridge: MIT Press, 173–204.

Farrar, Cynthia, James Fishkin, Donald Green, Christian List, Robert Luskin, and Elizabeth Paluck. 2010. "Disaggregating Deliberation's Effects: An Experiment within a Deliberative Poll," *British Journal of Political Science* 40(2): 333–347.

Fearon, James D. 1999. "Electoral Accountability and the Control of Politicians: Selecting Good Types Versus Sanctioning Poor Performance." In A. Przeworski, S. C. Stokes, and B. Manin, eds., *Democracy, Accountability, and Representation*. Cambridge: Cambridge University Press, 55–97.

Ferejohn, John, and Francis Rosenbluth. 2009. "Electoral Representation and the Aristocratic Thesis." In I. Shapiro, S. C. Stokes, E. J. Wood, and A. S. Kirshner, eds., *Political Representation*. Cambridge: Cambridge University Press, 271–303.

Fishkin, James. 2009. *When the People Speak: Deliberative Democracy and Public Consultation*. Oxford: Oxford University Press.

Fricker, Miranda. 2007. *Epistemic Injustice: Power and the Ethics of Knowing*. Oxford: Oxford University Press.

Galton, Francis. 1907. "Vox Populi." *Nature* 75 (March 7): 450–451.

Gardner, Howard. 1983. *Frames of Mind: The Theory of Multiple Intelligences*. New York: Basic.

Gastil, John, and Erik Olin Wright. 2019. *Legislature by Lot*. Verso.

Gigerenzer, Gerd. 2014. *Risk-Savvy: How to Make Good Decisions*. New York: Viking.

Gigerenzer, Gerd. 2008. "Why Heuristics Work," *Perspectives on Psychological Science* 3 (1): 20–281.

Goodin, Robert. 2005. "Sequencing Deliberative Moments," *Acta Politica* 40: 182–196.

Goodin, Robert, and Kai Spiekermann. 2018. *An Epistemic Theory of Democracy*. Oxford: Oxford University Press.

Goeree, Jakob K., and Leeat Yariv. 2011. "An Experimental Study of Collective Deliberation," *Econometrica* 79(3): 893–921.

Goodwin, Barbara. 1992. *Justice by Lottery*. Chicago: University of Chicago Press.

Grofman, Bernard, Guillermo Owen, and Scott L. Feld. 1983. "Thirteen Theorems in Search of Truth," *Theory and Decision* 15: 261–278.

Guerrero, Alex. 2014. "Against Elections: the Lottocratic Alternative." *Philosophy & Public Affairs* 42(2): 135–178.

Habermas, Jürgen. 1996. *Between Facts and Norms: Contributions to a Discourse Theory of Law and Democracy*. Translated by W. Rehg. Cambridge: Polity Press.

Harding, Sandra. 1998, *Is Science Multicultural?: Postcolonialisms, Feminisms, and Epistemologies*, Bloomington, Ind.: Indiana University Press.

Hong, Lu, and Scott Page. 2001. "Problem Solving by Heterogeneous Agents," *Journal of Economic Theory* 97(1): 123–163.

Hong, Lu, and Scott Page. 2004. "Groups of Diverse Problem Solvers Can Outperform Groups of High-Ability Problem Solvers," *Proceedings of the National Academy of Sciences of the United States* 101(46): 16385–16389.

Hong, Lu, and Scott Page. 2009. "Interpreted and Generated Signals," *Journal of Economic Theory* 144(5): 2174–2196.

Johnson, James. 2014. "Models Among the Political Theorists," *American Journal of Political Science* 58(3): 547–560.

Knight, Jack and James Johnson. 2011. *The Priority of Democracy: Political Consequences of Pragmatism*. Princeton: Princeton University Press.

Kuehn, Daniel. 2017. "Diversity, Ability, and Democracy: A Note on Thompson's Challenge to Hong and Page," *Critical Review: A Journal of Politics and Society* 29(1): 72–87.

Lhada, Krishna K. 1992. "The Condorcet Jury Theorem, Free Speech, and Correlated Votes." American Journal of Political Science 36(3): 617–634.

Landemore, Hélène. 2012. "Democratic Reason: The Mechanisms of Collective Wisdom in Politics." In H. Landemore and J. Elster, eds., *Collective Wisdom: Principles and Mechanisms*. Cambridge: Cambridge University Press, 251–289.

Landemore, Hélène. 2013. *Democratic Reason: Politics, Collective Intelligence, and the Rule of the Many*. Princeton: Princeton University Press.

Landemore, Hélène. 2014a. "Yes, We Can (Make it up on Volume): Answers to Critics," *Critical Review* 26(1–2): 184–237.

Landemore, Hélène. 2014b. "Democracy as Heuristic: The Ecological Rationality of Political Equality," *The Good Society* 23(2): 160–178.

Landemore, Hélène. 2015. "Inclusive Constitution-Making: The Icelandic Experiment," *Journal of Political Philosophy* 23(2): 166–191.

Landemore, Hélène. 2017. "Inclusive Constitution-Making and Religious Rights: Lessons from the Icelandic Experiment," *Journal of Politics* 79(3): 762–779.

Landemore, Hélène. 2018. "Referendums Are Never Merely Referendums: On the Need to Make Popular Vote Processes More Deliberative," *Swiss Review of Political Science* 24(3): 320–327.

Landemore, Hélène. 2020. *Open Democracy: Reinventing Popular Rule for the 21st Century.* Princeton: Princeton University Press.

Landemore, Hélène. 2021. "An Epistemic Argument for Democracy" in M. Hannon and J. de Ridder (eds), *The Routledge Handbook of Political Epistemology*. Routledge, 363–373.

Landemore, Hélène, and Jon Elster, eds. 2012. *Collective Wisdom: Principles and Mechanisms.* Cambridge: Cambridge University Press.

Landemore, Hélène, and Hugo Mercier. 2012. "Talking It Out With Others vs. Deliberation Within and the Law of Group Polarization" (first author, with Hugo Mercier), *Analise Social* 205(47): 910–934.

Ladha, Krishna. 1992. "The Condorcet Jury Theorem, Free Speech, and Correlated Votes," *American Journal of Political Science* 36(3): 617–634.

Lindert, Peter H. 2003. "Voice and Growth: Was Churchill Right?" *Journal of Economic History* 63(2): 315–350.

List, Christian, and Robert E. Goodin. 2001. "Epistemic Democracy: Generalizing the Condorcet Jury Theorem," *Journal of Political Philosophy* 9(3): 227–306.

Lupia, Arthur. 2006. "How Elitism Undermines the Study of Voter Competence," *Critical Review* 18: 217–232.

Lupia, Arther, and Matthew D. McCubbins. 1998. *The Democratic Dilemma: Can Citizens Learn What They Need to Know?* Cambridge: Cambridge University Press.

Manin, Bernard. 1997. *The Principles of Representative Government.* Cambridge: Cambridge University Press.

Manin, Bernard. 2005. "Democratic Deliberation: Why We Should Promote Debate rather than Discussion." Paper delivered at the Program in Ethics and Public Affairs Seminar, Princeton University, October 13.

Maskivker, Julia. 2019. *The Duty to Vote.* Oxford: Oxford University Press.

Matthijs, Matthias, and Blyth, Mark. 2018. "When Is It Rational to Learn the Wrong Lessons? Technocratic Authority, Social Learning, and Euro Fragility," *Perspectives on Politics*, 16(1): 110–126.

Medina, José. 2013. *The Epistemology of Resistance: Gender and Racial Oppression, Epistemic Injustice, and Resistant Imaginations.* New York: Oxford University Press.

Mercier, Hugo and Hélène Landemore. "Reasoning is for Arguing: Explaining the Successes and Failures of Deliberation," *Political Psychology* 33: 243–258, 2012.

Mercier, Hugo, and Dan Sperber. 2011. "Why Do Humans Reason? Arguments for an Argumentative Theory," Behavioral and Brain Sciences 34(2): 57–74.

Mokyr, Joel. 2016. *A Culture of Growth: the Origins of the Modern Economy.* Princeton NJ: Princeton University Press.

Mueller, Dennis C., Robert D. Tollison, and Tomas D. Willet. 2011. "Representative democracy via random selection." In P. Stone (Ed.), *Lotteries in public life. A reader.* Exeter: Imprint Academic.

Mulgan, Richard G. 1984. "Lot as a Democratic Device of Selection," *Review of Politics* 46: 539–560.

Ober, Josiah. 2008. *Democracy and Knowledge: Innovation and Learning in Classical Athens.* Princeton: Princeton University Press.

OECD. 2020. *Innovative Citizen Participation and New Democratic Institutions: Catching the Deliberative Wave.* Paris: OECD Publishing. https://doi.org/10.1787/339306da-en.

Olken, Benjamin. 2010. "Direct Democracy and Local Public Goods: Evidence from a Field Experiment in Indonesia," *American Political Science Review* 104(2): 243–267.

Page, Benjamin I., and Robert Y. Shapiro. 1992. *The Rational Public: Fifty Years of Trends in Americans' Policy Preferences.* Chicago: University of Chicago Press.

Page, Scott E. 2007. *The Difference: How the Power of Diversity Creates Better Groups, Firms, Schools, and Societies.* Princeton, NJ: Princeton University Press.

Page, Scott E. 2018. *The Model Thinker: What You Need to Know to Make Data Work for You.* New York: Basic Books.

Parkinson, John, and Jane Mansbridge. 2012. *Deliberative Systems: Deliberative Democracy at the Large Scale.* Cambridge: Cambridge University Press.

Pitkin, Hanna. 1967. *The Concept of Representation.* Berkeley: University of California Press.

Popkin, Samuel. 1994. *The Reasoning Voter: Communication and Persuasion in Presidential Campaigns.* Chicago: University of Chicago Press.

Przeworski, Adam. 2000. *Democracy and Development: Political Institutions and Well-Being in the World, 1950–1990.* Cambridge: Cambridge University Press.

Quirk, Paul J. 2014. "Making It Up on Volume: Are Larger Groups Really Smarter?" *Critical Review* 26(1–2): 129–150.

Sakai, Ryota. 2020. "Mathematical Models and Robustness Analysis in Epistemic Democracy: A Systematic Review of Diversity Trumps Ability Theorem Models," *Philosophy of the Social Sciences* 50(3): 195–214.

Salovey, Peter, and John D. Mayer. (1990) 1998. "Emotional Intelligence." In K. Oatley, J. M. Jenkins, and N. L. Stein, eds., *Human Emotions: A Reader.* Oxford: Blackwell Publishers, 313–320.

Schumpeter, Joseph A. 1942. *Capitalism, Socialism, and Democracy.* New York: Harper & Row.

Sen, Amartya. 1999. *Democracy as Development.* New York: Anchor Books.

Singer, Daniel J. 2019. "Diversity, Not Randomness, Trumps Ability." *Philosophy of Science* 86(1): 178–191.

Sintomer, Yves. 2007. *Le pouvoir au peuple: Jury citoyens, tirage au sort, et démocratie participative.* Paris: La Découverte.

Spencer, Weart. 1998. *Never at War: Why Democracies Will Not Fight One Another.* New Haven: Yale University Press.

Sternberg, Robert. J. 1985. *Beyond IQ: A Triarchic Theory of Human Intelligence.* New York: Cambridge University Press.

Stone, Peter. 2007. "Why Lotteries Are Just," *Journal of Political Philosophy* 15(3): 276–295.

Stone, Peter. 2009. "The Logic of Random Selection," *Political Theory* 37: 375–397.

Stone, Peter, ed. 2011. *Lotteries in Public Life: A Reader.* Exeter: Imprint Academic.

Sunstein, Cass. 2002. "The Law of Group Polarization," *Journal of Political Philosophy* 10(2): 175–195.

Sunstein, Cass. 2006. *Infotopia: How Many Minds Produce Knowledge.* London: Oxford University Press.

Surowiecki, James. 2004. *The Wisdom of Crowds: Why the Many Are Smarter than the Few and How Collective Wisdom Shapes Business, Economies, Societies, and Nations.* New York: Doubleday.

Taleb, Nassim. 2005. *Fooled by Randomness: The Hidden Role of Chance in Life and in the Markets.* New York: Random House.

Thompson, Abigail. 2014. "Does Diversity Trump Ability? An Example of the Misuse of Mathematics in the Social Sciences," *Notices of the American Mathematical Society* 61(9): 1024–1030.

Thompson, Dennis. 2008. "Deliberative Democratic Theory and Empirical Political Science," *Annual Review of Political Science* 11: 497–520.

Tong, Zhichao. 2020a. "The Imperative of Competition: Epistemic Democracy in the International Context." Dissertation defended at the University of Toronto, July 27, 2020.

Tong, Zhichao. 2020b. "Political realism and epistemic democracy: An international perspective," *European Journal of Political Theory* 19(2): 184–205.

Waldron, Jeremy. 1995. "The Wisdom of the Multitude: Some Reflections on Book 3, Chapter 11 of Aristotle's Politics." *Political Theory* 23(4): 563–84.

Wantchekon, Leonard. 2012. "How Does Policy Deliberation and Voting Behavior? Evidence from a Campaign Experiment in Benin." http://citeseerx.ist.psu.edu/viewdoc/download?doi=10.1.1.304.4095&rep=rep1&type=pdf

Warren, Mark E., and Hilary Pearse. 2008. *Designing Deliberative Democracy: The British Columbia Citizens' Assembly.* Cambridge: Cambridge University Press.

Weisberg, Michael. 2013. *Simulation and Similarity: Using Models to Understand the World.* New York: Oxford University Press.

Wittman, Donald. 1995. *The Myth of Democratic Failure: Why Political Institutions Are Efficient.* Chicago: Chicago University Press.

Part 3

RESPONSES

Chapter 9

Brennan: Response to Landemore

1. THE HONG–PAGE THEOREM IS TRIVIAL AND DOES NOT SHOW DIVERSITY TRUMPS ABILITY

Oxford debate books are fun to write because we, the authors, don't know exactly what the other person will say beforehand. They are thus like real in-person debates. When we read the other author's half, some of what they say we anticipated, and some surprises us.

I had expected Landemore to rely more heavily on, and supply more of, an empirical argument for open democracy and rely less on the Hong–Page "Diversity Trumps Ability" Theorem and variations thereof. However, her defense of democracy still rests on the Hong–Page model. Accordingly, while I offered some brief criticisms in chapter 2, I need to respond in greater depth here.

Let me summarize my main conclusions: The proof of the Hong–Page Theorem is trivial. Hong and Page do not actually "prove" that diversity trumps ability; instead, they largely *assume* it. The proof does not show what Landemore and others who use it say it says. It cannot be used to

Debating Democracy. Jason Brennan and Hélène Landemore, Oxford University Press. © Oxford University Press 2022. DOI: 10.1093/oso/9780197540817.003.0011

defend actual democracy from any of the problems with democracy I outline in chapter 1.

Let's start by describing Hong and Page's 2004 paper "Groups of Diverse Problem Solvers Can Outperform Groups of High-Ability Problem Solvers" in plain English. First, I'll examine the *assumptions* of their proof. Note, again, that these are the *assumptions* or *premises* of their proof. They do not prove or provide evidence for these claims. Note, also, that my list of assumptions does not correspond to their numbered list of assumptions. I'm including assumptions buried deeper down in their text but which they do not label as such.

1. They assume that all agents in collective decision have the same value function; that is, the same ranking/ ordering of possible outcomes from better or worse.

Ask yourself, is real-life democracy like this? Or do people have different value functions and different rank- ings of outcomes? Should democracy accommodate reason- able pluralism about values?

In the real world, agents making a collective decision usually have different values and thus rank different states of affairs differently. They do not agree on what counts as a solution to the problem and they often do not agree on what the problem is. Presumably, this will affect how much real people will listen to, defer to, or learn from each other. If you and I have different values, then what you regard as a solution or an improvement I might regard as indifferent or worse. For instance, if Stephan Macedo and I deliberate about a policy, he might regard it as a plus that it limits immigration, while I will regard that as a big minus.

The model does not imagine, let alone prove, that citi- zens who deliberate together will come to share the same values. Rather, it assumes at the outset that their values are the same.

Now, since I deny that justice is decided by fiat, I am not automatically troubled by the idea of using an objective value function. However, when we are modeling how agents deliberate and reason together, the unrealistic assumption that they will in fact share the same value function will make the model perform better than real-life deliberation and decision-making will. In real life, we disagree, and that changes whether we listen to or learn from each other.

2. They assume—not prove, but assume—that the problem these agents are trying to solve is so difficult that no agent can solve the problem alone.

At least this is not an unmotivated assumption. Many political problems are like that. What's the optimal monetary policy during a recession? I'd be inclined to trust a group of economists over any single one of them.

Still, there might be problems that an individual economist or philosopher can solve by herself, especially since, in the real world, she can piggyback or learn from others' previous work. Think of a single-authored paper that offers a policy solution to a problem.

We cannot invoke the Hong–Page Theorem to tell us that the group must outweigh the individual in such cases, because the theorem applies to cases where it is stipulated that no one person can solve the problem alone. Accordingly, while Hong and Page argue that many heads are better than few, the reason their theorem says two heads are better than one is in part because it assumes one head is never enough.

Let's move on.

3. They assume that every agent in the decision-making process has one and only one "heuristic" or method that she uses to try to solve the problem. They assume if that agent uses that heuristic, she then gets stuck on some answer, and she stays stuck until someone else helps her. They thereby assume that no agent has any internal "cognitive diversity"; they thereby assume that agents do not as individuals try out different problem-solving heuristics or techniques.

This is where the proof starts to get seriously problematic. Why would it be interesting or valuable to model each individual problem-solver as having only *one* heuristic or method to solve a problem? In the real world, high-ability and highly reliable agents have many problem-solving methods and heuristics. (This point is sometimes invoked in defense of democracy.) They have good ideas about how and when to switch them. For instance, I'm fluent in a variety of social scientific and philosophical approaches to analyzing social problems, and if you read my work, I flip between them all the time. Same with Landemore. We're not special or weird—most competent people are like that. Indeed, even incompetent or low-ability people have a range of problem-solving tools, heuristics, and methods they can use. But Hong and Page model all of their decision-making agents, both the low- and high-ability agents, as having only one way of approaching a problem and being unable to switch methods to improve their work.

This unrealistic assumption is problematic because it loads the dice against "high-ability" agents. The high-ability agents in their model are stipulated to have exactly one highly reliable but (stipulated to be) imperfect heuristic or problem-solving method, and when they get stuck, it's stipulated they can become unstuck when others help them.

4. They assume that whenever one agent gets stuck, there is "always" another agent who can improve upon the first by using a different heuristic. Here is the direct quotation from their paper:

Assumption 2 (Diversity).

$\forall x \in X \setminus \left\{x^*\right\}, \exists \theta \in \theta$ such that $\phi(x) \neq x$.

This assumption is a simple way to capture the essence of diverse problem-solving approaches. When one agent gets stuck, there is always another agent that can find an improvement due to a different approach.[1]

Again, notice that they simply *assume* that whenever one smart agent—an agent who by assumption can use only one method to solve a problem she cannot solve alone and can only get unstuck with help from others—gets stuck, then there is always another agent who can improve the situation by using a different approach. They don't prove this; it is rather a stipulation. But this seems like something they would want to prove, not assume. As we will see, this stipulation ends up making their proof question-begging.

Further, note that this is what they use the word "diversity" to signify. The word "diversity" here does not stand in for and is not analogous to or related to what your campus or corporate diversity officer means by "diversity." It does not mean or signify diverse racial or demographic

1. Hong and Page 2004.

identity, diverse values (on the contrary, they assume all agents rank things the same way), diversity of life experiences, diverse mental models, diverse memories, diverse categories and ideas, diverse conceptions of reality, diverse philosophies, or whatnot. It instead means "having a different heuristic or problem-solving method which can improve the solution to the problem."

Anyone using this theorem must be very careful (though they rarely are) not to equivocate, that is, not to treat the concept of "diversity" in the proof to correspond with 99% of what we mean by "diversity" in the real world. Unfortunately, Landemore's half of this book does this, for instance, in her discussion of different epistemic standpoints or in her discussion of how different demographic groups might have different kinds of knowledge or expertise. The Hong–Page Theorem's use of "diversity" has almost nothing to do with that. What "diversity" means in the theorem is not having a different point of view, but rather having a different problem-solving approach which by stipulation can improve the current outcome or decision.

So, to summarize, "diversity" in the "Diversity Trumps Ability" theorem does not mean what you think it means. And in order to prove that this so-called diversity helps group decision-making, Hong and Page assume rather than prove that there is always another person with another method or heuristic that can improve upon whatever anyone else does. In other words, diversity helps because they have stipulated that "diversity" refers to a thing that they have stipulated helps.

5. They assume all agents defer to other agents when those other agents can improve the group decision.

They assume agents always recognize when someone else has produced a better solution/improved upon the current best solution, and then always defer to that improvement.

Again, ask, in real-life group decision-making, do people uniformly do that? If one person's method improves upon what others have come up with, do they often, let alone always, recognize this as such and then defer to it? (See chapter 1: the answer is no.)

So, part of the reason the Hong–Page Theorem will "show" that group decision-making leads to improved decisions is that Hong and Page . . . assume that people always recognize and defer to the best answer on the table.

6. They assume there is always in principle a wide range of heuristics/methods that can be used to solve a problem, rather than just one or a few.

This assumption is less troubling than the others, but it may not always be true. Maybe some problems can only be solved with a few tools or with only one tool. I won't dwell on this point here.

7. They assume that the agents are trying to solve *one* problem.

In their paper, they model agents as trying to solve one problem rather than balancing multiple problems at once. We can reasonably ask whether this is a good way to describe what citizens are doing when, say, they vote or deliberate on policies. At any rate, the problems they model citizens as solving are highly simplified.

Those are some, if not all, of the questionable assumptions. Given all these assumptions, it then becomes trivial rather than interesting that when agents are tasked with solving a problem, they can improve decision-making by adding more heads. Granted, it still takes a mathematical proof involving computer simulations, and many critics think they go wrong there.

But, overall, what does proof actually say? Well, this: Assume that there is some problem everyone agrees on, both on what the problem is and what counts as a solution. Assume people have different levels of ability in solving that problem, but no one can solve the problem alone. Assume that everyone automatically accepts any improvement or better solution offered by anyone else. Assume that everyone, no matter how smart, uses one and only one method to solve the problem and can never on their own switch to new methods or heuristics. Assume that if anyone gets stuck, then there is always someone out there with a new method that can improve upon the current offered solution. (Again, this is what they call "diversity.") Well, then it follows that as we add more and more people to the group, then our chances of adding a person who will help (remember—we stipulated that these helpful people exist) become higher and higher. After all, they've *stipulated* that when we add people to the group, they can only do one of two things: either improve the group's decision or have no effect at all.

But, again, it gets worse. As I argued in chapter 2, even if the Hong–Page Theorem were not trivial, even if it meant what Landemore and others take it to mean, it would still not be much help in defending democracy. Why not? Consider this dialogue:

EMPIRICIST: Real-world group decision-making is beset by the following pathologies, as shown by seventy years' worth of studies.

APRIORIST: I have a mathematical model that says group decision-making *could* be excellent under certain circumstances, so your empirics are not troubling.

EMPIRICIST: How does your model deal with the problems I've described in the real world?

APRIORIST: My model simply *assumes* they do not occur.

EMPIRICIST: Oh, okay then.

These assumptions do not map onto stuff in real-life democracy. People have different value functions. Maybe one agent could solve a problem alone. In the real life, smart agents often use multiple methods to solve problems and switch methods when one fails. In real life, we certainly cannot assume there is always another agent who can improve our situation when we are stuck. What Hong–Page mean by "diversity" does not correspond to what we mean by "diversity" in real-life democracy or what Landemore discusses in her half of this book. In real life, people might not have diverse perspectives and they might not even be trying to solve the problem. In real life, people don't always or even usually recognize when others are doing better, nor do they automatically defer to them. In real life, adding more people to a group trying to solve a problem doesn't mean everyone in the group just accepts the best answer or evidence anyone else gives. If people are closeminded or tribalistic, if they are more concerned to wave flags than to solve problems, if they do not recognize or defer to superior solutions, if there is little actual cognitive diversity, if they are not trying to solve a problem when they "deliberate" or "vote," if people do not understand the problem or are beset by serious cognitive biases, this means the theorem does not apply. The theorem is not only trivial but also relies upon a description of group decision-making alien to what groups actually do in real-life democracies.

Now, while Landemore relies heavily on the Hong–Page Theorem as defended in the 2004 paper, I admit there are some other papers that try to prove similar points with relaxed assumptions, and thus with less trivial results. However, similar remarks will apply to these papers. Their models must in some way correspond with what actually happens in real-life voting or deliberation. They must not assume away pathologies but instead show how they can be overcome. The modeled concept of "diversity" or whatnot must correspond to actual cognitive diversity, such as differences into real people's mental states, beliefs, heuristics, and models. Otherwise, we get stuck with trivialities rather than real proofs, which at most show that "Democracy would be great it if worked differently from how it actually does."

Let's put the problem more generally: If you are trying to model decision-makers, the assumptions you impose determine whether "diversity" beats ability or vice versa. All this depends on the nature of the problem we stipulate, what kinds of methods we stipulate that agents use, whether we stipulate that agents learn from each other, might disagree, or might become dumber upon interacting with each other, whether we stipulate that they agree on what counts as a solution or not, and how much internal "diversity" we stipulate agents have. We can concoct scenarios in which twelve smart agents beat a larger group of 100,000 (which includes the original twelve) or in which 100,000 relatively dumb agents beat 10,000 smarter agents. It all depends on the assumptions we build into the model. The more important question will be which of these infinite models we construct best explains actual group decision-making in various contexts.

Instead of relying on a priori models of questionable application, here is what I recommend Landemore and others do. First, find a plausible way to operationalize and measure things like diversity and individual reliability. Find a plausible way to operationalize and measure the quality of various group decisions. Then do lots of empirical studies examining how diversity and individual reliability in different group decisions, with different decision rules, with different kinds of interactions, and with different composition, affect group outcomes. Then, given Landemore's extremely strong claims, show that there is no easy way to improve group decision-making through weighing votes differently, excluding the incompetent, selecting a diverse but also elite group, and so on. Then, I think, she'd have a strong case.

2. DOES VOTER IGNORANCE AND IRRATIONALITY MATTER? YOU ALREADY BELIEVE IT

Over seventy years of evidence, from countless surveys, psychological experiments, political science and economic analyses, and the like indicate that voters are ignorant and epistemically irrational about politics, largely innocent of ideology, but highly tribalistic and stubborn in their political attachments. Landemore does not attempt to debunk this evidence—how could she?—but claims it matters much less than I think it does. Instead, she challenges me to prove that it really does make democracy function worse. After all, I admit democracy outperforms . . . dictatorships, absolute monarchies, and totalitarian one-party states, but how could it do so if voters are so bad? She challenges me to identify the mechanism by which bad voting leads to bad outcomes.

Landemore seems to think she's put me into a quadrilemma. If I criticize voters' inputs into the democratic process, she'll then say I haven't *proven* these inputs definitively lead to defective outcomes. If I criticize the outcomes (for instance, voters' antipathy to free trade and immigration), she'll probably just say (as she does in her half) that I'm upset voters don't support my "libertarian" politics. If I point out, as I actually do when I make these supposedly libertarian arguments, that most economists Left and Right agree with me, she'll then say, so what, economists aren't always right. If, instead, I had written a 20,000-word literature review of what political scientists and economists have said about how exactly voters influence policy, she'd probably complain that any particular summary of that vast literature is controversial. So, for Landemore, there is no way for me to "win" regardless of how I argue.

For what it's worth, *Against Democracy* is not a libertarian book. Indeed, almost none of my published work on any subject is libertarian, even though I identify as a "bleeding heart libertarian." My criticisms of democracy do not rest on the particular outcomes or policies I support. If, due to brain injury or peer pressure, I suddenly became a Rawlsian Left-Liberal or a radical income egalitarian, I wouldn't have to modify my books or papers on democracy. They are in that way ideologically neutral.

That said, if readers want a specific *empirical* example of the dangers of democratic voting, I recommend my book *Injustice for All*, with Chris Surprenant. Among other things, we trace how the US's peculiar policy of voting for district attorneys, prosecutors, and, in many cases, judges, along with voter misinformation about crime rates and the effectiveness of prison, go a large way to explain why the US's criminal justice system is so dysfunctional, harsh, and punitive. Note that this claim—that part of the reason the US criminal justice system is so unusually harsh and punitive is that it is unusually democratic—is largely uncontroversial among scholars who study this issue. As I argued in chapter 3, even if a political system is democratic overall, it's often best that various parts of that system be administered in a non-democratic way.

Despite her arguments to the contrary, I suspect Landemore agrees with me that voter ignorance and irrationality matter, because she has to. One reason she has to is that, as I argued above and in chapter 2, if voters are tribalistic, pigheaded, and irrational, then they won't behave in the way the Hong–Page model needs them to behave in order for the theorem to apply. But beyond that, to deny my worries involves biting bullets the size of cannonballs. Let me illustrate by repeating and then expanding on some thought experiments from my half.

1. Imagine I have a magic wand. When I wave it, it will make nearly all voters 50% more ignorant, irrational, and tribalistic than they already are.

Ask: Would it be a bad thing to wave it? Would it hurt democratic performance? Would it lead to more injustice and worse outcomes? When I ask critics these questions, basically all of them say yes. I doubt Landemore would say that waving the wand would be fine, or that open democracy is so wonderful that it would overcome the perverse effects of the wand.

2. Imagine a world like ours, with the same kinds of political institutions, but in which voters were perfectly epistemically rational and perfectly well-informed. Now imagine I brandish a second magic wand. When I wave this wand, I will transform these cognitively perfect citizens, and instead make them as ignorant and irrational as the actual living citizens of the US or France today. (You can reread chapter 1 for a review of how bad such voters are.)

Ask: Would it be horrible to wave that wand? Would it hurt democratic performance, and lead to more injustice and worse outcomes? When I ask critics these questions, basically all say yes. I doubt Landemore would say that waving this wand would be fine, or that open democracy is so wonderful that it would overcome its perverse effects.

3. Imagine I have a third magic wand. When I wave it, it will greatly improve today's existing voters' ignorance and irrationality; it will make them 50% more informed about both basic political facts and whatever theories are needed to understand those facts, about how to predict what policies will do, and so on. It will reduce their cognitive biases by 50%.

Would it be a good thing to wave it? Would it help democratic performance? Would it lead to more justice and better outcomes? When I ask critics these questions, basically all of them say yes. I doubt Landemore would disagree.

To say that waving a wand in cases 1 and 2, or refusing to wave it in case 3, would not make any real difference, one must either be radically pessimistic or radically optimistic about democracy. Maybe Landemore is just such an optimist on the basis of the Hong–Page Theorem, though, as we just saw, there are few grounds for optimism.

Instead, I think Landemore would admit that waving wands 1 and 2 would be horrible while waving wand 3 would be wonderful, regardless of which kind of democratic system—lottocracy, open democracy, representative democracy—we have. But if so, then we are no longer debating *whether* political ignorance and irrationality matter, but *how much* they matter and what the precise relationship is between political outcomes and voters' inputs into that system.

There is plenty of reasonable empirical debate in political science about how exactly voters influence policy, but I needn't hang my hat on any particular view. The less you think voters influence policy, the less you should care about my complaints, but then you start having to bite big bullets you don't want to bite. (For example, if, according to you, voters don't influence policy much, then by hypothesis suppressing or disenfranchising all black voters would have little effect on how well politicians serve black citizens' interests. Do you want to say that?) If you think voters have significant influence, then their irrationality and ignorance matter, unless somehow aggregating their votes washes most or all of the bias and ignorance out. But as we discussed in chapter 2, there is no reason to think that.

Further, given Landemore's own celebratory understanding of the Hong–Page Theorem, she must say this stuff matters too. Voters must behave in certain ways for the Hong–Page Theorem to apply to their collective decision-making. If they are extremely unsophisticated, if they lack sufficiently robust and detailed mental models, if they lack good problem-solving heuristics, if they lack diverse perspectives and instead apply the same heuristics or models or simply parrot the beliefs of others, if when they are voting or deliberating they aren't really trying to solve the problem but are instead engaging in conspicuous displays of loyalty to their tribe or simply trying to raise the status of one group over others, and so on, then the Hong–Page model either fails or works badly. The Hong–Page Theorem (on her understanding) does not say that cognitive abilities, bias, and ignorance do not matter; it simply says that adding diverse problem-solving heuristics can sometimes help the group even more than increasing individual reliability.

3. WHY DO DEMOCRACIES PERFORM SO WELL?

Landemore challenges me by asking me to explain why democracies perform as well as they do, given all their supposed pathologies. It's a good question, but I don't think it's a stinger.

Part of the issue is that we are comparing democracies to the other forms of government we've tried, which mostly include one-party totalitarian states, absolute dictatorships, military juntas, slave societies, and dictatorships. The bar is low. Nevertheless, democracies generally perform much better than these other, terrible forms of government. So, saying the bar is low is important, but we still need to know why they raise the bar as high as they do.

Part of the reason is that democracy historically has come bundled with *other* institutions which do almost all the work. A condensed and simplified, but still accurate history of modern democracy would go as follows: During the Enlightenment, it become popular to think that people should be granted strong decision-making over their own lives. Support for economic and civil liberalism become widespread. Democratic republicanism came along as part of the package, as theorists and politicians at the time who pushed for liberal reforms saw democratic republicanism as a kind of extension of the liberal idea into the realm of politics.

Liberalism was a miracle that greatly enriched and improved the lives of every place it touched. Perhaps democracies perform well because they are liberal, not because they are democratic per se. As partial evidence of this, it seems that societies that are democratic but not liberal perform worse than societies that are liberal but not very democratic.[2] We can rate countries by how democratic they are or how liberal they are, and then run regressions examining the relationship between various institutions and various outcomes (life expectancy, income, etc.) while controlling for the confounding effect of other institutions.

---

2. Brennan 2016b; Jones 2020; Acemoglu and Robinson 2013.

Liberal economic and social arrangements greatly improve people's lives; democracy, as an independent variable, less so.

I think that bad voter behavior leads to unjust government and harmful policies. But I also don't want to overstate that. One reason democracy works is that it doesn't work—that is, politicians, technocratic bureaucracies, and so on, have significant freedom to act independently of what the voters "want" without fear of being "punished" by "retrospective voting." (As I argued in chapter 1, voters don't really want much and don't engage in much retrospective voting.) While I would not dare suggest that politicians are do-gooder public servants, nevertheless, they are generally fairly well-informed compared to the masses, and have some incentive to do what is good for the polity rather than what merely sounds good. Martin Gilens makes a similar point in his own work. He notes that politicians are much more likely to side with voters at the ninetieth percentile of income than those in the middle or bottom. As a small-d democrat, he is partly horrified by this, because it suggests that voters are not really equal. But as a liberal, he is partly relieved, because if other voters got their way, this could be horrible. Gilens finds that high-information Democrats have systematically different policy preferences from low-information Democrats. He notes that high-income voters are also generally high-information voters, while middle- and low-income voters are generally low-information voters. High-income Democrats tend to have high degrees of political knowledge, while poor Democrats tend to be ignorant or misinformed. Poor Democrats approved more strongly of invading Iraq in 2003. They more strongly favor the Patriot Act, of invasions of civil liberty, torture, protectionism, and of restricting abortion rights and access to birth control. They are less tolerant of homosexuals and more opposed to gay rights.[3] I hope that if I say that the Patriot Act, the Iraq War of 2003, invasions of civil liberty, torture, protectionism, and restricting abortion rights and access to birth control are bad, Landemore won't dismiss this by saying that's just my "libertarian" politics talking.

4. OPEN DEMOCRACY

My favorite part of Landemore's argument is her defense of open democracy. I favor experimenting with new forms of governance that might reduce the systematic flaws in democracy as we find it. I'm glad she does too.

Open democracy combines the lottocratic idea advanced by Claudio López-Guerra[4] and Alexander Guerrero[5] and along with various forms of public deliberation. For the reasons I articulated in my chapter 2, I am not nearly as optimistic about deliberation as many democrats; the empirical results are underwhelming.[6]

That said, I find Landemore's defense of open democracy puzzling for at least two reasons. First, as you can see from her half of this book, she is skeptical about criticisms of democracy that hold that voter ignorance and irrationality lead to worse political outcomes. Landemore seems skeptical of my—or anyone else's—claims that democracy

3. Gilens 2012, 106–111.
4. López-Guerra 2011.
5. Guerrero 2014.
6. Myers and Mendelberg 2013.

underperforms or makes unjust choices. Yet in order to motivate the need for open democracy on instrumentalist grounds, she has to appeal (very briefly) to defects in the structure of existing representative democracies which in turn cause them to underperform, and at the same time she must insist these defects are entirely about how representatives and others act, rather than how voters act. Insofar as she admits voters act in defective ways and that this causes bad, unjust, or even suboptimal policy outcomes, she then will have difficulty claiming that democracy with everyone voting always outperforms any epistocratic alternative. She will have to admit, instead, that epistocracy could in principle work better than representative democracy. Perhaps she could then argue that in the real world we would bungle it too badly to derive any real benefit.

Second, the models of open democracy she defends involve selecting a small subset of citizens at random who will then make political decisions. But if, as Landemore insists, more heads are always better than fewer, why limit ourselves to this small subset?

López-Guerra and Guerrero defend lottocratic systems in which a small number of randomly selected citizens are charged with deciding policy matters in a small domain (e.g., trade policy) for a few years. But they explicitly do so because they think that creating such citizen councils, with a small number of voters, will change voters' incentives. Their votes will suddenly matter and so they will be incentivized to overcome their ignorance and bias.

But Landemore cannot avail herself of this reasoning without conceding that I am right that real-life democracy is full of ignorant, biased, and irrational voting and that such voting makes things worse. At best, it seems, she can say that the epistemic returns to adding more voters to her lottocratic councils are sufficiently small that it's not worth the opportunity cost of appointing them.[7] Working on councils takes time and effort that could be spent elsewhere.

7. For a formalization of this point regarding Condorcet's Jury Theorem, see Brennan 2011.

Chapter 10

Landemore: Response to Brennan

DESPITE THE AVALANCHE OF FACTS that Jason Brennan brings against the average voter, he does not prove anything conclusive against democracy as a regime form itself. This is so in large part because the simplistic "garbage in, garbage out" model he relies on is invalid. We simply cannot conclude all that much from voters' limited competence in answering decontextualized (and elitist) questionnaires about the epistemic properties of democracy as a collective decision procedure. And indeed, in the end, Brennan concedes, democracy is still the best regime around, no matter how flawed. On this, we agree. In the limited space I have to respond, I would like to expand on two other points of agreement and two points of disagreement.

1. DEMOCRACY VERSUS THE MARKET

I agree with Brennan that everything should not be decided politically and that more democracy is not the

Debating Democracy. Jason Brennan and Hélène Landemore, Oxford University Press. © Oxford University Press 2022. DOI: 10.1093/oso/9780197540817.003.0012

answer to everything. The question of the relevant domain of politics versus that of the market, in particular, is a question of great interest and one that I did not have much to say about in this debate. That's because, for me, it only makes sense to compare a regime form with another regime form and to do so for a given background domain of questions. The market is *not* a regime form and when it came to comparing democracy versus non-democratic alternatives, I assumed throughout a similar, predefined domain of questions. By opening the domain question, Brennan has initiated a different, orthogonal debate pitting the question of the best regime versus the question of the limits of government. Or, to put it differently, the question of collective agency versus that of individual freedoms and rights. Or, to put yet another way, the question of collective, conscious decision-making, where the responsibility and accountability of agents (whether individual or collectives) can be identified, versus that of unconscious market processes that are the non-intentional results of individual actions geared toward their private interests. So I concede that "if for a given issue, *all* forms of political decision-making are inferior to non-political methods, then that issue should stay outside the scope (at least presumptively) of politics" (Brennan 2016). But for me this question is off topic relative to the goal of this volume—which was to debate democracy as a regime formed and not to debate the more general question of "Where should politics end and the market begin?"—which could be posed in the context of *any* regime.

2. THE FLAWS OF EXISTING DEMOCRACIES AND THE NEED FOR MORE, OPEN-MINDED EXPERIMENTATION

I agree with some of Brennan's criticisms of existing democracies. I also agree with his call for more experimentation and his claim that we have a duty to fix democracy as we know it. I just doubt that his solution—a combination of mini-publics defining the relevant questionnaire to administer to voters and the enlightened preference approach that he borrows from Bryan Caplan—is the best we can do from a purely instrumental point of view (barring the fact that this solution is hardly empowering of all equally and thus not democratic).

On purely instrumental grounds I doubt his solution would work because it assumes that the relevant questions can be defined apart from and ahead of a process of political problem-solving in context (e.g., the very act of ruling). One lesson from the French Citizens' Convention for Climate is that the participants could only mobilize the relevant knowledge in the very process of trying to identify and propose solutions to curb French greenhouse gas emissions in socially fair ways. This knowledge was both organically identified and generated in a back and forth between citizens themselves and between citizens and the experts available to consult. This is why, ultimately, deliberation among citizens, on the basis of expert knowledge, seems to me a much more promising solution than Brennan's hyper-rationalistic and convoluted system, where we need first to identify the correct set of questions voters should be able to answer and then build a virtual electorate based on it. Letting a mini-public define the relevant knowledge is certainly less elitist than Caplan's earlier proposal to define it against the benchmark of economics PhD holders' knowledge and preferences. However, Brennan's solution still depends on the illusion that there is such a thing as a one-size-fits-all set of preferences and views that can be identified ahead of an actual deliberative process.

3. ON THE VALUE OF DELIBERATION

Jason Brennan is extremely skeptical of the epistemic value of deliberation as a way to improve democracy, essentially because of the empirical claims of a few social scientists like Cass Sunstein or Tali Mendelberg (five of Brennan's arguments against deliberation can be traced in footnotes to that latter author alone). He criticizes my optimism about deliberation on the grounds that I adduce for it the admittedly quirky example of Iceland. Yet, strikingly, Brennan himself, like me, counts on deliberation among randomly selected citizens as one key element of his preferred solution. Brennan justifies this co-optation of deliberation by saying that unlike regular deliberative democrats, who are too optimistic about the problem-solving capabilities of citizens, all he asks of citizens in his deliberative model is for them to name and identify the relevant knowledge, not to actually acquire and use it.

In reply note first that many deliberative experiments do not require participants to acquire much knowledge at all so Brennan's modest proposal does not stand out for originality in this respect. For example, the Icelandic

National Forum 2010 asked 950 randomly selected citizens to identify the common values they wanted to see embedded in a new constitutional document. This task did not require acquiring new knowledge but simply mobilizing their intuitive understanding of what it meant to be an Icelander.

Second, many other deliberative experiments ask citizens to mobilize their "situated" or "user knowledge" (their lived experience of the laws and economy they live under), which is also not a taxing cognitive task. For example, the randomly selected assemblies of the French Great National Debate of 2019 asked citizens to identify salient problems in society and the kind of solutions to them that they would expect at a very general level. Since this task took place over a day and a half, participants had no time to learn anything new or consult experts.

It is true, though, and maybe these are the examples Brennan has in mind, that some deliberative processes involve gaining and mobilizing expert knowledge and are in that sense extremely demanding of citizens. This was the case of the 2004 British Columbia Citizens' Assembly on electoral reform or the 2019–21 French Citizens' Convention for Climate, which is to date the most ambitious process in terms of scope and complexity of the problem citizens had to address and which involved the participation of over 140 experts. The Irish Citizens' Assemblies of 2012 and 2016, respectively on same-sex marriage and abortion, were at an intermediary level of difficulty. For example the Citizens' Assembly on abortion exposed participants to presentations by doctors and women having gone through an abortion, asking citizens to process a new kind of technical and experiential knowledge.

So there is a range of options in deliberative democracy in terms of what can be asked of citizens. Brennan's proposal falls neatly under an already existing category of Citizens' Assembly. But more importantly, when it comes to cognitively demanding deliberative experiments, what we find is that citizens as a group are, in fact, contrary to Brennan's predictions, capable of producing complex, nuanced proposals, such as an electoral reform project in Canada, a brand new constitutional text in Iceland (a less trivial task than Brennan makes it sound), or 149 extremely detailed legislative proposals on how to reduce greenhouse gas emissions in the case of the French Convention for Climate. Brennan complains that in the Icelandic case citizens "weren't being asked to write fine policy details on a hard question, such as what the optimal way to regulate diesel emissions." Well, in the French this is exactly what citizens were asked to do. In fact, they had to do something even harder because not only were they asked about ways to reduce greenhouse gas emissions by 40% of their 1990s levels by 2030. They were asked to do so "in a spirit of social justice" adding a layer of moral complexity to a technically already complicated task. Granted, the French Convention was given a budget of five million euros, nine months, and access to multiple experts. But the point is that they succeeded. And why should deliberative democracy come cheap or not rely on experts? The empirical evidence is in fact a lot more promising than Brennan acknowledges or is aware of.

4. PAYING PEOPLE TO KNOW

I would finally like to share a more tentative disagreement about Brennan's proposal "to pay people to know." As intriguing as it is, I don't think this commodification of knowledge acquisition would work.

Note first that in practice, in mini-publics where people receive financial compensation, the payment is never aimed at incentivizing them to know anything. It is meant instead to incentivize them to come and use their brains on complicated issues for a few days, a few weeks, or, sometimes, months. As a result, I'm not sure that citizens would score much higher on the tests that Brennan has in mind post-deliberation just because they are paid to know. Nor does it matter that much if they don't. We all know that knowledge fades quickly, as does memory. Do we really want citizens to learn to the test, cramming the night before like bad students? Conducting interviews with participants, I am struck by how little they remember of things that they discussed in great detail when I observed them over many weekends. Their answers, a few weeks later, are vague and much less informed than their exchanges were during the sessions. What matters, it seems to me, is that in the moment of the deliberation citizens mobilize their unique perspective, their critical faculties, as well as whatever knowledge they have in their short-term, working, and long-term memory and can process at the relevant moment. But while some amount of knowledge is thus necessary, it need not be the sort of generalist knowledge Brennan has in mind. We should pay people not to store content permanently in their brain—a task we have long outsourced to Google—but to compensate them for the time and energy they spend *mobilizing* whatever knowledge they have; processing knowledge made available to them in the moment; and using their judgment, imagination, and creativity in the deliberative process. That is what collective intelligence is about. Collective intelligence is an emergent, living, constantly evolving thing—not necessarily something that can be identified and quantified ex ante, or measured as a specific kind of knowledge permanently and statically lodged in individuals' brains.

Finally, the idea of "paying people to know things" commodifies something that does not even need to be commodified for people to engage in it, namely learning, which is the process through which we get to know things. Human beings are endlessly curious creatures for whom learning about new things is usually pleasurable. Economic theory tells us that promising monetary rewards for this kind of tasks actually diminishes the motivation for it, crowding out what are the real powerful motors of human action, namely intrinsic motivation. It seems to me that paying people to compensate them for their time away from family, work, etc. is a good thing to do. But paying them "to know" is likely to diminish their likelihood of learning anything in the first place. So all in all, while I appreciate Brennan's effort to think up new ways of improving our flawed democracies, I really don't think his solutions are either democratic enough or workable.

INDEX